# TOO BUSY *NOT* TO PRAY

## Slowing down to be with God

**Bill Hybels**

Adrianna Riemersma

Inter-Varsity Press
Norton Street, Nottingham NG7 3HR, England
*Email: ivp@ivpbooks.com*
*Website: www.ivpbooks.com*



*First published 1988*
*Second edition 1998*
*Third edition 2008*

British Library Cataloguing in Publication Data

A catalogue record for this book is available from the British Library.

ISBN: 978-1-84474-305-6

Set in Monotype Dante 12/15pt
Typeset in Great Britain by Servis Filmsetting Ltd, Stockport, Cheshire
Printed and bound in Great Britain by Ashford Colour Press Ltd, Gosport, Hampshire

Inter-Varsity Press publishes Christian books that are true to the Bible and that communicate the gospel, develop discipleship and strengthen the church for its mission in the world.

Inter-Varsity Press is closely linked with the Universities and Colleges Christian Fellowship, a student movement connecting Christian Unions in universities and colleges throughout Great Britain, and a member movement of the International Fellowship of Evangelical Students. Website: *www.uccf.org.uk*

To Joel Jager
a lifetime friend

CONTENTS

# INTRODUCTION TO THE TWENTIETH-ANNIVERSARY EDITION

Twenty years ago I reached a breaking point. I'd been a Christ-follower for more than a decade, Willow Creek was growing like a weed and in many regards the future looked bright – divinely bright even. But despite all the inspiring dynamics unfolding around me, my prayer life was gasping for breath. I knew the importance of prayer. I knew how to pray. And I even wanted to pray. I just didn't pray, at least with the frequency and intensity I knew I should.

Determined to improve my own prayer disciplines, I delivered a sermon series on the subject. (I thought I'd drag as many people from Willow as possible along with me on the journey.) The series was well received and was eventually made into the book you are holding. I had no idea at the time that God would let this material hang around for so long, but I'm grateful for the run it continues to have. I'm sure part of the reason is that many of the big ideas God initially gave me for *Too Busy Not to Pray* are classic concepts, immune from the effects of time.

Although I hope I've matured in my prayer life since then, I still find myself returning to the simple practices of maintaining a consistent time and place to pray (chapter 5); organizing my prayers according to tried-and-true frameworks, such as ACTS (chapter 6); and listening for the Spirit's promptings in my day-to-day quest for direction and wisdom (chapter 14). Not only has shoring up my prayer life improved my relationship with God, but as solid prayer practices have taken root, I've noticed my personal relationships reaching new levels of effectiveness as well.

For many years now, I've been travelling extensively on the international front. This often requires the use of translators, which can slow down the communication process dramatically. It's something that frustrates me more than I should let it, but it's amazing how prayer has served to bridge cultural divides, including the ever-present language barrier.

When I finish speaking in some faraway land, a line of people often forms that's full of those who want to chat about what God is up to in their lives. On most occasions my translators have already packed up and headed home for the night, so I suggest with hand motions that we pray to God instead of trying to hack our way through an exasperating exchange.

Back and forth, in our native tongues, we talk to God. And even though we have no idea exactly what the other person is praying for, we know beyond the shadow of a doubt to whom we are praying. As a result of talking to the One we both consider to be all powerful, all knowing, all caring, all loving and all attentive to our prayers, we walk away from the conversation sensing a close bond in Christ. Pretty amazing.

Recently I have sensed God calling me to dive deeper into helping address societal ills that threaten us today. If you've seen extreme poverty face to face – if you've held the hand of someone dying of HIV/AIDS, or stood beside food lines filled with families needing nourishment, or stumbled upon children who call a pavement their bed – then you know how overwhelming the needs are. Take an honest assessment of the awful situations all around, compared with our relative ability to do anything about them, and you are most likely left feeling hopeless and helpless and scared.

But here again prayer shows up and provides a bridge from despair to hope, from fear to confidence and, most critically, from spectating to participation. Chapter 16, 'The needs around us', was born out of my genuine desire to help Christ-followers (including me!) get off the bench and into the game as it relates to fighting injustice in all its forms. I believe God has a role for each of us to play, if only we'll quieten the mind, bend the knee and take time to discover it.

I keep a prayer journal and frequently I'll flip to the early pages to see what I was praying for during those days as well as how my prayers were answered. It's always interesting to reflect on how the hand of God moved a mountain or calmed a sea on my behalf. And in my estimation there is no taller mountain looming, no stormier sea raging right now than the one called injustice. For Christ-followers who are as fired up as I am about righting the wrongs of a broken world, there is no better first step to take than prayer. I hope you'll keep this type of big, world-changing vision at the front of your mind as you work through the chapters that follow.

Twenty years ago LaVonne Neff was instrumental in transforming my original sermon series into something immensely more readable, and Ashley Wiersma helped me to freshen things up for this twentieth anniversary edition. I'm grateful to them both. I am thankful also for the thousands of faithful, rank-and-file pray-ers I've met over the years. Your persistence in making your needs known to God, and your diligence in listening for and acting on his replies, inspires me more than you'll ever know.

I often wonder what would transpire if every Christ-follower got serious about installing solid prayer practices into their lives. What kind of kingdom gains do you suppose would be made if each of us made pressing into God through prayer a non-negotiable part of our everyday experience?

I believe hearts would soften. Habits would shift. Faith would expand. Love for the poor would increase. Positive, purposeful legacies would be built. And a ravenous hunger would rumble through us all to get usable and to get used in significant ways by the one true God.

We can make this happen in our lifetime, friend. And it all starts with learning, and loving, to pray.

# GOD CALLS US INTO HIS PRESENCE

# 1. GOD OF PEACE, GOD OF POWER

Prayer is an unnatural activity.

From birth, we learn the rules of self-reliance as we strain and struggle towards independence, and frankly, prayer flies in the face of all that. It is an assault on human autonomy, an indictment on self-sufficient living. To people like me, who are fond of racing down the fast lane, determined to make it on their own, prayer can seem a really annoying interruption.

Although prayer is alien to our proud human nature, somehow, at some point along life's journey, most of us fall to our knees, bow our heads, fix our attention on God and just plain pray. We may look both ways to be sure no-one is watching; our knees may creak at the foreignness of the activity; but still, we pray. It's as if something within us is hard-wired with the knowledge that in so doing we weave stronger threads of intimacy with the One who alone can provide peace to endure and power to overcome whatever challenges we face.

## Drawn to an intimate relationship

Ask people who have suffered tragedy or trial, heartbreak or grief, failure or defeat, loneliness or discrimination. Ask what happened in their souls when they finally fell to their knees and poured out their hearts to the Lord.

Such people have told me, 'I can't explain it, but I felt God understood me.' Others have said, 'I felt surrounded by his presence,' or, 'I felt a comfort and peace I'd never felt before.'

Many years ago my dad – still relatively young and an extremely active man – died of a heart attack. As I drove to my mother's house in Michigan after getting the news, I wondered how I would continue to function now that the person who believed in me more than anyone else was gone.

That night in bed I wrestled with God. 'Am I going to recover from losing my father? Why did this happen? How can I put it all together in my mind and in my life? If you really love me, how could you do this to me?'

Suddenly, in the wee hours of the morning, it was as if I had turned a corner and was now headed in a new direction. God simply conveyed, 'I'm able. I'm enough for you. Right now you doubt I have a purpose in all of this, but please . . . trust me.'

That experience may sound far-fetched, but what occurred as a result of it was unmistakable. After that tear-filled and despairing night, I was never again tortured by doubt – either about God's care for me or about my ability to handle life without my dad. Grief, yes. My father's death wounded me deeply, and I will always miss him. But it did not set me adrift without anchor or compass. Even to this day, that was the bleakest night I have ever known. But as if intent on piercing my darkness, God utterly overpowered me with a massive beam of courage, reassurance and hope.

More recently, consistent prayer thwarted one of those dark

nights of the soul. My daughter, Shauna, was pregnant with my first grandchild. The whole family, myself included, eagerly anticipated the arrival of this little person. But in unguarded moments I found myself weighed down by wondering about complications with Shauna or her baby.

The only thing I knew to do was to pray – intentionally, continuously and with great faith. There was no other way to cope with the level of concern only a father can feel for his daughter. I told God what I was worried about. Then I handed over my worries and left them there with him. He seemed a lot more composed about the whole thing, which relaxed me immensely. Each time he and I went through this little ritual, after several minutes of focused prayer, I could feel the sense of burden or foreboding being lifted from my body. Shortly thereafter a sense of peace would be restored to my inner world.

Surely something similar was what caused the apostle Paul to write to the Christians at Philippi, 'Do not be anxious about anything, but in everything, by prayer and petition, with thanksgiving, present your requests to God. And the peace of God, which transcends all understanding, will guard your hearts and your minds in Christ Jesus' (Philippians 4:6–7).

What relief there is in God-ordained peace!

## Prayer's best by-product

Prayer has not always been my strong suit. For many years I knew far more about prayer than I ever practised in my own life. I have a racehorse temperament, and the tugs of self-sufficiency and self-reliance have always been very real to me. Taking time to practise prayer meant wilfully veering off the fast track I was on – a move I wasn't sure I wanted to make.

But during those hair-on-fire days, the Holy Spirit gave me a spiritual nudge – a prompting of sorts – so direct that I couldn't ignore it, argue against it or disobey it. The prompting was to explore, study and practise prayer until I finally understood it. 'I know about your whole racehorse thing,' he said (well, not audibly), 'but this is something I'm asking you to do.'

I obeyed that prompting by reading fifteen or twenty major books on prayer, some old and some new. In addition, I studied almost every passage on prayer in the Bible. Classic verses on prayer, in particular, had a profound impact on me.

- 'The LORD is near to all who call on him, to all who call on him in truth.' (Psalm 145:18)
- 'Ask and it will be given to you; seek and you will find; knock and the door will be opened to you.' (Matthew 7:7)
- 'I waited patiently for the LORD; he turned to me and heard my cry.' (Psalm 40:1)
- 'If you believe, you will receive whatever you ask for in prayer.' (Matthew 21:22)

When I reached the end of all that diligent study, I did something radical: I prayed. It has been more than thirty years since that self-imposed masterclass on intercession, and still my prayer life soars. Most of the time.

During the flows and the ebbs, however, I remember that the most fulfilling by-product of a life of prayer is not the satisfaction of ticking off a daily to-do list – perfect attendance in your prayer room doesn't always equal deep fulfilment. The most fulfilling by-product is also not receiving miraculous answers to the actual prayers prayed, although those are wonderful when they occur. What I have discovered along the path of prayer-life cultivation is that the greatest thrill to a life of prayer is the qualitative difference made in one's relationship with God.

God and I used to be rather casually acquainted with one another. We just didn't get together and chat all that often. But now we engage in substantial, soul-searching conversations for a good chunk of time every morning, we 'replay the tapes' as the day comes to a close and we talk on the run every hour in between.

Naturally I have come to know God a whole lot better since I slowed down to pray. I have been astonished by his approachability, endeared by his care, stilled by his presence, encouraged by his affirmation and challenged by his insatiable desire to make the truth known. Nothing compares to this type of first-hand knowledge of God.

Given the fact that you're holding this book, perhaps the Holy Spirit is leading you to learn more about prayer too. If so, you are about to embark on an amazing adventure! As you grow in prayer, God will reveal more of himself to you, breathing more of his life into your life. Mark my words: this will be the most fulfilling and rewarding part of your experience with prayer, more so than your diligence or even his faithfulness. Accepting, trustworthy, peace filled, grace giving – these character traits of God will be made more vibrant to you as you devote yourself to cultivating a life of prayer.

## A channel for God's power

Through prayer God gives us his peace, which is one reason why even self-sufficient types fall on their knees and pour out their hearts to him. We pray because, by intuition or experience, we understand that perfect peace comes only through relating with the Peacemaker himself.

But there is another reason. People are drawn to prayer

because they know that God's power flows primarily to people who pray.

The miracles of Israel's exodus from Egypt and journey to the Promised Land were all answers to prayer. So were Jesus' miracles of stilling storms, providing food, healing the sick and raising the dead. As the early church formed and grew and spread throughout the world, God answered the believers' continual prayers for healing and deliverance.

God's power can change circumstances and relationships. It can help us face life's daily struggles. It can heal psychological and physical problems, remove marital obstructions and meet financial needs. In fact, this supernatural power can handle any kind of difficulty, dilemma or discouragement – a topic we'll explore further in chapter 3, 'God is able.'

Someone has said that when we work, we work, but when we pray, God works. His strength is available to praying people who are convinced to the core of their beings that he can make a difference. Sceptics may argue that answered prayers are only coincidences, but as an archbishop once observed, 'It's amazing how many coincidences occur when one begins to pray.' How true this is!

## Hands raised to heaven

More than any other biblical passage, one story in the Old Testament has persuaded me that prayer yields significant results. It is found in Exodus 17:8–13, which says this:

> The Amalekites came and attacked the Israelites at Rephidim. Moses said to Joshua, 'Choose some of our men and go out to fight the Amalekites. Tomorrow I will stand on top of the hill with the staff of God in my hands.'
>
> So Joshua fought the Amalekites as Moses had ordered, and Moses, Aaron and Hur went to the top of the hill. As long as

> Moses held up his hands, the Israelites were winning, but whenever he lowered his hands, the Amalekites were winning. When Moses' hands grew tired, they took a stone and put it under him and he sat on it. Aaron and Hur held his hands up – one on one side, one on the other – so that his hands remained steady till sunset. So Joshua overcame the Amalekite army with the sword.

In this scene Israel's most renowned leader is faced with a crisis. An enemy army intent on wiping out Israel has just arrived near Israel's desert camp. Moses calls in his most capable military leader for a strategy discussion. After a thorough planning session, Moses announces the approach they will take.

'Joshua,' he says, 'tomorrow you take the best fighting men we have, lead them out on the plains to meet the enemy and fight with courage. I am going to take two men with me, climb the hill that overlooks the plains and raise my hands towards heaven. I'm going to pray that God will pour out courage, coordination and supernatural protection on our troops. Then I'm going to watch and see what God does.'

## God's power released

Because he believes in the power of prayer, Joshua goes along with Moses' plan. He'd rather have Moses' prayer support than his military support any day of the week.

The men head into battle, and when Moses' hands are stretched heavenwards, Joshua's troops prevail, fighting with a divine intensity that drives back the enemy. But Moses' arms eventually grow weary. He drops them to his sides and walks around the hill, viewing the battle from all sides. To his horror, the tide shifts right before his eyes. Joshua's troops are being struck down; the enemy is gaining a foothold.

Moses stretches his arms towards heaven again and brings the matter to the Lord. Immediately the momentum shifts back to Joshua and the Israelites, and once again they drive the enemy back. And then it occurs to Moses: if I want to open the floodgate for God's supernatural intervention to flow on the battlefield, I'd better keep my hands open towards heaven in prayer!

Moses discovered that day that God's prevailing power is released through prayer. When I began praying in earnest, I also concluded that if I am willing to invite God to involve himself in my practical challenges, I will experience his prevailing power – in my home, in my relationships, in my church, in my leadership roles, wherever it is most needed.

Friend, the same is true for you.

The power you receive directly from the hand of God may come in the form of wisdom – an idea you desperately need and can't come up with yourself. It may come in the form of courage greater than you could ever muster on your own. It may come in the form of confidence or perseverance, uncommon staying power, a changed attitude towards a spouse or a child or a parent, altered circumstances, maybe even outright miracles. However it comes, God's prevailing power is released in the lives of people who pray.

There is, however, another and more sobering side to the equation. It is hard for God to release his power in your life when you put your hands in your pockets and say, 'Thanks, but no thanks. I can handle things on my own.'

Pocket stuffers, beware: don't be surprised if one day you get the nagging feeling that the tide of battle has shifted against you and that you're powerless to do anything about it.

Prayerless people cut themselves off from God's peace and from his prevailing power, and a common result is that they feel overwhelmed, overrun, beaten down, pushed around and defeated by a world operating with a take-no-prisoners approach. It's surprising to me how many are willing to settle for lives like that. Don't be one of them! Nobody has to live this way. Prayer is the key to unlocking God's consistent and prevailing power in your life.

Whatever battles you face, look to God for your strength and your peace. Not because I say so, but because the Bible does (in Psalm 29:11, to be exact: 'The LORD gives strength to his people; the LORD blesses his people with peace').

## Keep the power flowing

Once Moses made the connection between prayer and God's power, he determined to spend the rest of the day praying for God's involvement in the battle. But his arms grew weary. He knew better than to drop them to his sides; he had done that before and watched his troops get wiped out as a result. So Aaron and the other man who accompanied him up the hill found a stone Moses could sit on. Then each man crawled under an arm and helped Moses hold his hands to the heavens. What a picture – Moses being supported by caring people who wanted to help him keep the power flowing! Suffice it to say, Israel won the battle that day.

My hope is that this book will play the role of a man like Aaron in your life, a companion that can help you hold up your arms so that supernatural power keeps flowing in you until the day is done and the victory is yours. I'd like it to be used by God to inspire you to pray, whether for the first time this hour or for the first time ever. His ears are wide open to you, and his peace and power are yours for the asking.

# 2. GOD IS WILLING

Over the course of thirty-plus years in ministry, I've run into far too many people who are convinced that the two greatest challenges associated with prayer are getting God to listen to them in the first place and then finding the lost key that will unlock the vault of blessings that God for some reason would prefer not to open. The God they know is apparently so busy keeping the cosmos in order that he has zero interest in hearing about their petty problems. Maybe he does care about the lilies and the birds and the cattle on a thousand hills, but there is no way he'll take care of real people.

If you fall in line with this interpretation of things, you have been deceived. The idea that God doesn't care about his children is rooted in a lie, plain and simple. The truth of the matter is that God is anything but reluctant to hear from his children. We don't need to pester our way into his presence, as many people believe. What's more, we can rest assured that he is quite interested in taking care of us! We mean far more to him than a bunch of cud-chewing bovines wandering about on a hillside. We are the crown of his creation!

## The desperate widow

During his earthly ministry, Jesus once told his disciples a story to help them understand God's willingness to hear the prayers of his children and to act on their behalf. It's recorded in Luke 18:2–5, which reads:

> In a certain town there was a judge who neither feared God nor cared about men. And there was a widow in that town who kept coming to him with the plea, 'Grant me justice against my adversary.'
>
> For some time he refused. But finally he said to himself, 'Even though I don't fear God or care about men, yet because this widow keeps bothering me, I will see that she gets justice, so that she won't eventually wear me out with her coming!'

In today's world, despite the often overwhelming difficulties involved in being a widow, many of these women are able to rise to positions of affluence and influence. They are allowed to work, attend school and own property. What's more, most widows are able to maintain their social status without being cast aside simply because they have lost a spouse. But this was not the case in the Middle East two thousand years ago.

In Jesus' day a widow generally had no education, no job, no money, no property, no status and no power. Her survival was critically linked to whether or not she had a son, a father or a brother-in-law who would agree to care for her. If not, she would probably become a beggar – the first-century equivalent of a homeless person. Regardless, she'd forever remain a social outcast to those in her community.

To make an already challenging situation far worse, the

widow in Jesus' story also faced a human adversary. Although the text doesn't reveal what type of harassment she suffered (physical? emotional? the withholding or stealing of funds that should have been used for her support?), she was battling some sort of villain from her home town . . . and losing.

The widow had no good way to protect herself, no relatives to see her plight and offer help and no governmental organization to come to her aid. She had only one shot at warding off this bully and that was to go before a local judge, plead her case and throw herself on his mercy. This is precisely what she decided to do.

## The unjust judge

Jesus describes the judge she would encounter in two crisp statements: he did not fear God and he did not respect other human beings (Luke 18:2).

Without fear of God, the judge had no sense of accountability. He did not respect God's Word, God's wisdom or God's justice, and he seemed to have no appreciation for the fact that on a future day of reckoning he would be required to give an account for his actions. As a result, he made his own justice and decreed whatever suited his fancy. Like a loaded cannon loose on deck, he fired wherever and at whomever he wished.

Without respect for other human beings, the judge didn't care one iota about how his decisions affected the people who sought justice in his courtroom. Since people didn't matter to him, he felt free to use and abuse them. He saw them not as brothers and sisters but as irritating problems, interruptions, headaches and hassles.

This was the type of person who would serve as the widow's last resort.

If she'd had any friends, I'm sure they would have shouted, 'Go to court? Don't waste your time! That judge is probably in cahoots with your enemy. He'll laugh in your face and toss you out before you know what hit you.' (Which is exactly what the judge did, except that the story doesn't end there.)

Still, the widow persevered, went before the judge and not surprisingly was summarily dismissed. Hurt and shocked by his behaviour, the widow gathered her wits and examined her situation once more. She steeled her confidence: 'I don't have any other options. Cruel and unsympathetic though he may be, this judge is my only hope. Somehow I've got to convince him to protect me.'

The question that remained was how.

There was no higher court that would hear her case. Penniless, she couldn't even bribe the judge. 'I know what I'll do', she thought. 'I'll pester him. Every time that judge turns around, I'm going to be right in his face. I'll follow him home, to work, to the racetrack, whatever. I'll be on him like a shirt until he offers me protection, puts me in jail or does away with me altogether.'

Her inventiveness paid off. The widow beleaguered the judge until the day finally came when he raised the window in his office and shouted to the listening world outside, 'I can't stand it any more! Somebody fix this woman's problem. I don't care what it takes – just do it! She's driving me crazy.'

In the end the crooked, uncaring judge finally gave the widow protection from her adversary. It was a move born not out of the goodness of his heart but out of her extraordinary talent for being . . . well, annoying.

But his motivations are hardly the point of this story.

## Meaning misunderstood

Unfortunately, many Christ-followers have been taught that the meaning of the story is the exact opposite of what Jesus intended.

Luke 18:1 says Jesus told this story to show his disciples 'that they should always pray and not give up'. Many readers get that far in the text and stop, which causes them to make a grave error in interpreting it. Thinking of it as an allegory, they look at the tale this way:

We humans are the widow. Impoverished, powerless, with no connections and no status, we are unable to handle our problems alone and feel that we have nowhere to turn.

God, then, must be the judge, these misguided readers continue. He's not really interested in our situation. After all, he has a universe to run, angels to keep in harmony, harps to tune. It's best not to bother him unless it's really important.

If we're desperate, though, we can always do what the widow did: we can annoy him. Bang on the doors of heaven. Spend hours on our knees. Ask our friends to bug him too. Sooner or later we may wear him down and wrench a blessing from his tightly closed fist. Eventually he will shout, 'I can't stand it any more – somebody fix this problem! Whatever it takes, just do it. This person is driving me crazy!'

Honestly, now, does that sound like the God you know?

So, what does the story mean? Thankfully Jesus himself interpreted it as soon as he finished telling it. According to him, this story is not an allegory, where elements in the story stand for truths outside the story. Instead it is a parable – a short story with a puzzling aspect that forces listeners to think. And this particular parable is a study in contrast.

### You, as opposed to the widow

Friend, you are not like the widow. Neither am I. In fact, we are the exact opposite of her. She was poor, powerless, forgotten and abandoned. She had no relationship with the judge. For him, she was just one more item on his to-do list.

You and I, on the other hand, are not abandoned; we are

God's adopted children, Jesus' brothers and sisters. We are in God's family and we matter to him. So don't tiptoe into God's presence, trying to find the secret of attracting his attention. Just say, 'Hello, Father,' and know that he absolutely loves to hear your voice.

My dad was a busy man who travelled all over the world. When he was in the office, it could be a challenge to get past the switchboard and secretaries to reach him. For this reason he gave a few select business partners, his wife – and us kids – his private number. We knew that no matter how busy he was, we could call him at any time and be sure of reaching him. He loved to hear our voices that much!

These days I also have a private line that rings at my desk. I've given the number to a few colleagues to use in emergencies, and I've given it to my wife and children. I've told my children they can call me at any time for any reason. Believe me, no voices sound sweeter to me than theirs. When I hear 'Hi, Dad', I don't care what I'm juggling. It can drop. My children are top priority to me.

## God, as opposed to the unrighteous judge

In Luke 18:7–8, we read, 'Will not God bring about justice for his chosen ones, who cry out to him day and night? Will he keep putting them off? I tell you, he will see that they get justice, and quickly.'

The judge in Jesus' story was crooked, unfair, disrespectful, uncaring and preoccupied with personal matters. Which is the polar opposite of the God we serve. Can you imagine a child of God calling his private line and hearing brutal statements like, 'I'm busy right now. I don't want to hear about your job troubles, your family struggles, your financial woes.' Or, 'Don't bother me with your personal needs. I want to take care of everyone . . . except you. If you really want to help me, then go and figure this thing out on your own.' Or, 'Not to be rude or anything, but that's enough whining! Blah, blah, blah . . . can you please just cut to the chase?'

If one of my children ever called me and said, 'Dad, please, please, please, I beg you, I petition you, I plead with you to listen to my humble request,' what would be my reaction?

I'd say, 'Hang on, I don't like the underlying assumption here. You don't have to go through all those verbal gymnastics. What in my life is more important than you? What gives me greater pleasure than meeting your needs? Just tell me, what can I do for you?'

Now, take a father's feeling for his children and multiply it exponentially, and you'll know how your heavenly Father feels about you. No-one's voice sounds sweeter to God than yours. Nothing in the cosmos would keep him from directing his full attention to your requests.

God is interested in your prayers because he is interested in you. Whatever matters to you is a priority for his attention. Nothing in the universe matters as much to him as what is going on in your life this day. You don't have to pester him to get his attention. You don't necessarily have to spend hours on your knees or flail yourself or go without food to show him that you really mean business. He's your Father and he wants to hear what you have to say.

'Come into my presence,' our God conveys. 'Talk to me. Share all your concerns. I'm keenly interested in you because I'm your Father. I'm able to help because all power in heaven and earth is mine. I am willing to listen, and I am hoping to hear your voice!'

Friend, your God is righteous and just, holy and tender, responsive and sympathetic. He is willing – anxious even – to hear from you. Moreover, he is willing to act on your behalf.

## The God I know is willing to act

One of the most theologically enlightening experiences of my life occurred many moons ago, when my son, Todd, was just a child. I bought him a BMX bicycle, which just about sent him over the edge of joy. I had never seen him so excited! After watching him ride it up and down the driveway that first afternoon, I had tears in my eyes when I walked back into the house. I said to my wife, Lynne, 'If that bike had cost five times as much, it would have been worth every penny. I've never received more joy from giving a gift to anyone!'

I got goose pimples watching him ride that bike that day, seeing his eyes wide with excitement. Right then and there, I started making plans to buy him a Harley Davidson one day – and a car! The sky was the limit for that boy because he was my son. Truth be told, it's still that way today.

I'm sure my tendencies in this arena stemmed from the way my dad brought me up. Once I was capable of handling his possessions properly, I had access to anything my father owned. One of his prized possessions was a forty-five-foot sailing boat. When I was in my early teens, my dad would say to me, 'Why don't you get one of your friends, hitchhike out to South Haven and take the boat out?'

Once my brother and I had our driving licences, Dad was equally generous with the car. And whenever he bought a new car, the first thing he did when he came home was to give us each a set of keys and say, 'Take it for a spin. If you want to take it out on a date, go ahead.'

My dad didn't read textbooks to get these feelings. Nor did I. They are just there. I'm unabashedly crazy about giving gifts to my children. And over time I have come to understand that it gives God great joy to bestow resources and power on his children too.

## Our generous Father

Most fathers love to be generous with their children. Jesus understood this, and that is why he pointed to examples of fathers to explain God's generosity in Matthew 7:9–11:

> Which of you, if his son asks for bread, will give him a stone? Or if he asks for a fish, will give him a snake? If you, then, though you are evil, know how to give good gifts to your children, how much more will your Father in heaven give good gifts to those who ask him!

Do you see the picture Jesus is painting? The son has been out in the fields working all day. By the time he comes home, he's famished. The family is at the table and dishes of steaming, fragrant food are being passed around. Can you imagine a father who would toss the boy a rock and say, 'Here, gnaw on this'? Or worse, one who would toss him an angry snake? No earthly fathers are perfect; we are all tainted with sin. Even so, we all recognize such behaviour as cruel. Good fathers want to give good gifts to their children – and so does our heavenly Father.

All through the Old Testament we see the theme that God is ready and willing to share his resources with his people. In the New Testament the concept is extended and made even more precious. There we learn that we have been adopted as God's sons and daughters and have become heirs, along with Jesus Christ, of his glorious kingdom.

- Jesus taught us to call God Father, *Abba*, which means, 'Papa'.
- The most repeated prayer in the Christian church is The Lord's Prayer, which begins with the words 'Our Father'.

- Ephesians 1:5 tells us that in love God 'predestined us to be adopted as his sons through Jesus Christ'.
- Galatians 4:7 says that if you are a Christ-follower, then you 'are no longer a slave but a child, and if a child then also an heir, through God' (NASB).
- In Romans 8:16–17, Paul writes, 'The Spirit himself testifies with our spirit that we are God's children. Now if we are children, then we are heirs – heirs of God and co-heirs with Christ, if indeed we share in his sufferings in order that we may also share in his glory.'

What a fantastic promise! God will cover us with blessings because he has adopted us as his sons and daughters. As God's children and legal heirs, we own the world and the universe. Should we ever fear to tell our Father our needs?

For some reason, though, most of us have a hard time accepting the gifts God gives us. In the past, when God would bless me with a special portion of his Spirit, a material item I had been wanting or a warm new relationship, I would be thinking, 'God must have had his wires crossed. Why would he do that for me?' In fact, I would feel guilty about my good fortune, as if I had somehow acquired something that God didn't really want me to have.

Over time I've learned to give God a little credit. If an egotistical judge was willing to hear from a widow of no status, how much more will our heavenly Father crane his ear from his celestial seat to hear our requests? If imperfect, earthbound fathers love to bestow blessings on their children, imagine how our perfect Father in heaven must delight in giving good gifts to us!

The Bible teaches that we serve a God who is simply looking for opportunities to pour out his blessings on us. It's as if he were saying, 'What good are my resources if I don't have anyone to share them with? Just give me a reasonable amount of cooperation, and I will pour out my blessings on you.'

This theme shows up in the Bible in at least three spots. Let the words of Scripture wash over you now.

> If you follow my decrees and are careful to obey my commands, I will send you rain in its season, and the ground will yield its crops and the trees of the field their fruit. Your threshing will continue until grape harvest and the grape harvest will continue until planting, and you will eat all the food you want and live in safety in your land.
>
> I will grant peace in the land, and you will lie down and no-one will make you afraid. I will remove savage beasts from the land, and the sword will not pass through your country. (Leviticus 26:3–6)

> All these blessings will come upon you and accompany you if you obey the LORD your God:
>
> You will be blessed in the city and blessed in the country.
>
> The fruit of your womb will be blessed, and the crops of your land and the young of your livestock – the calves of your herds and the lambs of your flocks.
>
> Your basket and your kneading trough will be blessed.
>
> You will be blessed when you come in and blessed when you go out.
>
> The LORD will grant that the enemies who rise up against you will be defeated before you . . .
>
> The LORD will open the heavens, the storehouse of his bounty, to send rain on your land in season and to bless all the work of your hands. You will lend to many nations but will borrow from none. (Deuteronomy 28:2–7, 12)

> Taste and see that the LORD is good. (Psalm 34:8)

Once and for all, let's trade in the notion that we have to plot and scheme to pilfer a blessing from God, somehow tricking him into giving up what he would rather keep for himself. The reality is that our God is good. It's in his nature to be good; it's who he is – a giving God, a blessing God, an encouraging God, a nurturing God, an empowering God, a loving God. This is the God who willingly waits for your call.

# 3. GOD IS ABLE

If you could ask God for one miracle in your life, knowing with 100% certainty that he would grant your request, what would you ask for?

Would you ask for your marriage to be put back together? Or for a situation in your job to change? Would you plead for a straying son or daughter to return? Or for a loved one to surrender to Christ? Would you pray for regained health – in your body, in your finances, in your prayer life?

Whatever your request might be, do you regularly and diligently, every single day, bring it to God in prayer, trusting that he will intervene in your situation?

## Can God handle it?

Most of us would admit that we don't pray often about our deepest needs. We grow faint of heart. We begin to pray, but we soon find our minds wandering, and we realize we're using empty phrases. Our words sound hollow and shallow and we start to feel hypocritical. Soon we give up altogether because it seems better to live with almost any difficult situation than to continue to pray ineffectually.

In our nobler moments we reach out to God because we know he is holding out loving arms towards us. But then we often fall back and try to face our difficulties in our own power. At some basic and perhaps unconscious level, we doubt whether God really can make a difference in the light of the problems we face.

So, even if we believe that God loves us and wants to help us, the question remains: is he able to do so?

For forty years my country, the USA, has been drowning in a sea of red ink, the federal deficit dogging us at every turn. The gap has widened between the rich and the poor, CEOs pull down princely salaries while mass layoffs multiply, unskilled workers cannot find jobs with decent pay and public aid fails to stem the tide of urban poverty. In spite of the dangerous economic and social situation, however, not one person has ever petitioned me to do something about it – and with good reason. I don't have any power to effect change in national policy that would solve our economic woes. In fact, even though the problems grow more serious every day, it would be a colossal waste of your time to ask me to try. Which is precisely why nobody ever does!

Parts of our world are perennially torn by war and civil strife. In the Middle East, parts of Africa (such as Uganda, Sudan and Somalia) and areas in South-east Asia and Colombia, government corruption, a disregard for human rights and a readiness to use force when words fail all contribute to the significant loss of human life every year. But again, no-one has ever asked me to do a thing about these deplorable situations. Why? Because even though it is desperately needed, I obviously have no power to bring about peace on earth.

### Believing in the heart

Many of us have pressing personal needs and serious problems that ravage our lives, but we neglect to ask God for help. Somewhere, far beneath our surface layer of faith and trust, we don't actually believe God has the ability to do anything about them.

The fact is, of course, that God is capable of handling any problem we could possibly bring to him. Creating planets didn't seem to be much of a problem for him. Neither was raising the dead. Nothing is too difficult for God to handle, but we won't see much proof of this until we actually ask him to handle it.

I used to make excuses for my faint-hearted prayer life, such as rationalizing my lack of perseverance in prayer with the idea that I didn't have any decent role models in this area to follow. 'I have too many responsibilities to fulfil,' I'd also think, trying to convince myself. 'There's no way I have the time to pray properly.'

But God convinced me that I was not being honest with myself. The real reason why my prayers were weak was that my faith was weak.

In my head I have always believed in God's omnipotence. I write about it and preach about it. But too often this belief hasn't registered where it really counts – in my heart. And when my heart is not persuaded, I don't pray about difficult situations. I don't ask God to meet my most pressing needs.

During my summer study breaks, I spend several hours a day reading, planning and praying in a small room that overlooks the harbour in South Haven, Michigan. For some reason one morning, as I watched the waves lap at the shore, a thought hit me regarding what the problem was in my prayer life. In my heart I did not believe that God could do anything about the messes all around me. I wanted to believe he was able. I just didn't.

Admitting this to God was embarrassing, but in the end it was cleansing.

I decided I didn't want to stay where I was, for all practical purposes disbelieving God's omnipotence. I launched an assault on my own lack of conviction, starting by opening my Bible and locating almost every passage that emphasizes God's ability to accomplish anything he desires.

### God's power over nature

I looked first at passages that demonstrate God's power over nature.

Exodus 14 and Joshua 3 prove that when God decided certain seas or rivers needed parting, he parted them. Exodus 16 and John 6 prove that when his people were hungry, he dropped food from heaven or multiplied bread and fish. Mark 4 says that when a storm endangered the lives of his disciples, he stilled it. And Joshua 10 assures us that when Israel's troops needed more time to consolidate their gains, he even extended the hours of daylight on the earth.

One story I especially liked came from Exodus 17:1–7. Moses had become frustrated because his people were thirsty. So he brought their need for water to God, and God said, 'See that rock?'

I can imagine Moses saying, 'Yes, but what does that have to do with water? If we need water, shouldn't we be looking at the ground?'

God answered, 'I don't want you and your people thinking you stumbled across some artesian well. I want you to know the power of the One you serve. I want you to experience my power over nature first-hand by sending you water right out of the side of that dry rock.'

And indeed he did.

I read and re-read all those stories about God's power over nature until I was convinced once again that they really did happen in actual time and space. What reassurance I found there!

## God's power over circumstances

Next, I looked at God's power to change impossible circumstances.

When the Holy Spirit came to the believers at Pentecost, many went out and preached that Christ had come back from the dead and was the Saviour of the world. As a result, thousands of people were converted to the new Christian movement. It made both the Roman officials and the traditional Jewish leaders a bit nervous; threatened by the crowds' enthusiastic response to the Christian preachers, they feared losing their authority over them.

And so the Roman and Jewish leaders resisted the movement. First, they arrested several prominent Christians and scolded them publicly. Which did no good at all; the Christians said they couldn't help speaking about what they had seen and heard.

Next, the officials captured, tortured and imprisoned some of the disciples. This had no lasting effect either. Once released, the disciples spoke with even greater boldness about Christ.

Finally, Herod Agrippa, Jerusalem's governor, arrested the apostle James, the brother of John, and had him executed. Acts 12 recounts the fact that he then laid plans to put Peter to death as well.

Unfortunately for Herod, he had Peter arrested during the Passover feast. Respecting Jewish traditions, he did not want to execute the apostle during Passover week, so Peter was slated to spend several days in jail before losing his head. To be sure that other Christians wouldn't spring their leader from the jail, Herod made Peter's security extra tight. Sixteen Roman soldiers were assigned to guard him. One was chained to his left wrist, one to his right. Sentries guarded the entrance to the cell.

Peter's fellow Christians did not get together to plan a prison break. They knew that any human tactics would be futile. Instead they prayed. But Peter remained in jail and his trial date approached.

## Astonished at the answer

The evening before the scheduled trial and execution, the Christians met at the home of Mary, the mother of John Mark, to hold an all-night prayer vigil. Peter, confident in Christ whether he lived or died, slept between his captors. Acts 12:7–10 explains what happened next:

> Suddenly an angel of the Lord appeared and a light shone in the cell. He struck Peter on the side and woke him up. 'Quick, get up!' he said, and the chains fell off Peter's wrists.
>
> Then the angel said to him, 'Put on your clothes and sandals.' And Peter did so. 'Wrap your cloak around you and follow me,' the angel told him. Peter followed him out of the prison, but he had no idea that what the angel was doing was really happening; he thought he was seeing a vision. They passed the first and second guards and came to the iron gate leading to the city. It opened for them by itself, and they went through it. When they had walked the length of one street, suddenly the angel left him.

Baffled, Peter looked around him. 'Is this real? Am I free? Has an angel really opened those prison doors?' When the truth dawned on him, he made a beeline for the house where the believers were gathered.

A servant girl answered his knock. Hearing his voice, she squealed with joy and ran back to tell the praying saints that their prayers were answered.

> 'You're out of your mind,' they told her. When she kept insisting that it was so, they said, 'It must be his angel.'
>
> But Peter kept on knocking, and when they opened the door and saw him, they were astonished. (Acts 12:15–16)

The first Christians were no more inclined than contemporary Christians are to think that God would miraculously rearrange circumstances in answer to prayer. But they prayed anyway. And God rewarded their incomplete faith, not by sending them comforting visions, but by altering history.

## God's power over the human heart

I then looked at passages that reveal God's power to change people's hearts.

God had the power to make shy Moses a leader (Exodus 3 – 4), to soften cruel Pharaoh's heart (Exodus 11:1–8), to keep discouraged Elijah from quitting (1 Kings 19:15) and to turn the fanatical persecutor Saul into a globetrotting apostle (Acts 9:1–31).

Looking again at the apostle Peter, we see the tremendous difference God's power made in his life. While imprisoned, Peter was so full of faith and peace that he could sleep deeply, even though he thought he would be killed the next day. Ten or fifteen years earlier, Peter had been a very different man.

When Jesus was captured in the middle of the night and

dragged before religious and civil authorities, most of the disciples ran away in terror. To his credit, Peter followed his Master right into the high priest's courtyard. But there he lost heart. 'They're going to kill him,' he thought, 'and then they'll start looking for his friends. I'd better put on a pretty good act.'

And so Peter, fearing for his life even though no-one had threatened it, tried unsuccessfully to alter his accent and persuade a group of servants that he had no connections with Jesus.

Jesus knew Peter would deny him. But he also knew that through God's mighty power Peter the coward would become Peter the rock – according to Matthew 16:18–19, the first major leader of the Christian church. 'Simon, Simon,' Jesus said to Peter on the night of the arrest and denial, 'Satan has asked to sift you as wheat. But I have prayed for you, Simon, that your faith may not fail. And when you have turned back, strengthen your brothers' (Luke 22:31–32).

After the crucifixion, Peter was a broken man who couldn't put the pieces of his life and his heart back together. Only God's power could change him. And indeed it did, as we see throughout the book of Acts.

I studied God's power in human lives, and once again I was convinced that God had his way whenever he desired – in the life of anyone he desired to change. History proved it.

## The same yesterday, today and for ever

I studied all these passages because I didn't want simply to agree with the doctrine of God's omnipotence (I already did that); I wanted to own it, which is a different matter altogether. I wanted to be able to say, 'I don't care what other people think. I don't care about scholars' opinions. I believe that God has shown his omnipotence factually, in history.'

But while it's one thing to own the doctrine of God's omnipotence in history, it's yet another to own the doctrine of his omnipotence today, in my home town, over my problems and concerns. To believe this, I must believe that God does not change, that he is immutable.

The doctrine of God's immutability is firmly established by biblical passages such as Malachi 3:6 ('I the LORD do not change') and Hebrews 13:8 ('Jesus Christ is the same yesterday and today and for ever').

God has not changed. He is not growing old and his power is not waning. Isaiah 40:28 asks,

> Do you not know?
> Have you not heard?
> The LORD is the everlasting God,
> the Creator of the ends of the earth.
> He will not grow tired or weary.

If he once was able to control nature, change people and alter circumstances, he remains able to do these things.

God is able – the Bible repeats this truth over and over. He was able to save three of his followers from a fiery furnace in Daniel 3. He was able to save Daniel from the lions' mouths three chapters after that. He was able to conceive a child in a ninety-year-old womb, Romans 4 testifies. He was able to give his followers all they could possibly need, says 2 Corinthians 9. He was able to save completely those who come to God through Jesus, according to Hebrews 7. And he is 'able to do immeasurably more than all we ask or imagine', if we believe the words of Ephesians 3.

God is able. Just as God has branded that truth into my heart, I have branded those words into a block of wood that I keep where I can see it as I kneel to pray each day. I value the reminder because making requests of God is an exercise in futility if I don't think he's actually able to answer.

Whatever it takes for you to own the doctrine of God's omnipotence, do it. Because once you own it, you migrate from being a faint-hearted pray-er to being an outright prayer warrior. And it's in that state that you begin to live out your belief that God has the power to do anything, to change anyone and to intervene in any circumstance.

## Your personal invitation

I hope you saw in chapter 2 that God is eager to pour his good gifts out upon us. And now I hope you realize that not only is he willing, but also he is able to bless you beyond your wildest imagination. If you find yourself still hanging back, reluctant to crash uninvited into the presence of the King of the universe, then hang back no longer! God, through Christ, has issued you a personal invitation to call on him at any time. In fact, it is impossible to come into his presence uninvited, because his Word tells us to 'pray continually' (1 Thessalonians 5:17).

If you have not yet surrendered your life to Christ, Jesus' invitation from Matthew 11:28–29 is this: 'Come to me, all you who are weary and burdened, and I will give you rest. Take my yoke upon you and learn from me, for I am gentle and humble in heart, and you will find rest for your souls.'

Once you choose to follow Christ, you may pray about anything: 'Do not be anxious about anything, but in everything,' Philippians 4:6 says, 'by prayer and petition, with thanksgiving, present your requests to God.' And you need not be timid in making those requests! Check out what Hebrews 4:16 has to say on the matter: 'Let us then approach the throne of grace with confidence, so that we may receive mercy and find grace to help us in our time of need.'

When you accept God's invitation, my friend, miracles begin to happen. You won't believe the changes that will occur in your life – in your marriage, your family, your career, your health, your ministry, your willingness to point people towards faith in God – once you are convinced in the core of your being that God is willing, that he is able and that he has invited you to come before his throne and do some serious business in prayer.

# GOD INVITES US TO TALK WITH HIM

# 4. HEART-BUILDING HABITS

Some time ago I was helping a friend grieve over the sudden loss of his dad. During the course of our conversation, he said, 'You must have been totally shocked when your own dad died at such an early age.'

'Well, yes and no,' I replied. 'The morning my brother called and told me our dad had just died of a heart attack – that was a shock. But that he would die young came as no surprise at all.'

My father's death was predictable because he had a horrendous family history of heart disease. Even more telling, though, were his terrible health habits. He used to say, 'I don't eat anything that hasn't been cooked in thirty-weight Havoline motor oil.' He never exercised. He didn't have regular hours for sleep. And he was in a fast-paced, high-stress job for his entire adult life.

Because of the lifestyle he chose, he suffered from indigestion, heartburn and high blood pressure. He consistently carried twenty extra pounds, couldn't walk at a fast pace and experienced serious dips in energy on a daily basis. Near the end of his life, he couldn't even do the basic sail-handling chores on his beloved boat. His bad habits not only led to an early death, but they also made for an uncomfortable life.

## The quest for the magic wand

Our spirits, like our bodies, have requirements for health and growth. Some people don't want to pay the price of developing good spiritual habits. Sadly, they end up paying the much higher price of spiritual disease and even death.

Last year a man came to me in despair, explaining that he had lost his job and had been searching for work unsuccessfully for months. But unemployment was not his worst problem. 'I feel so alone in this,' he said. 'Nobody in the church cares. Sometimes I don't even think God himself cares. I feel totally hopeless and helpless.'

I asked the man about his spiritual habits. Was he taking responsibility for feeding his faith? How often did he commune with God and listen for his heart on certain matters? Did he regularly attend church services? Was he maintaining friendships with any spiritually minded people? Was he reaching out to help meet others' needs, even as he had so many needs of his own?

No, the man said, he was doing none of these things. 'I just can't find the time,' he admitted. I subtly reminded him that, being unemployed and single, he was probably richer in time than in any other resource. He gave me a look I've seen before, one that seemed to say, 'Hey, did you miss the part about my problems? The last thing I need when I'm down on my luck is a list of to-dos from a pastor-type.'

That man wanted someone to wave a magic wand over him that would afford him an instant dose of strength and courage and peace. He wanted God's presence in his life; he just didn't want to form any habits that would actually cause it to show up.

When we make a habit of prayer, we stay constantly tuned to God's presence and open to receive his blessings. So, how do we make prayer a habit? Jesus laid out a few principles. But before we discuss them, I offer these two warnings.

## Caution 1: Avoid straitjacket discipline

First, if you are one who loves lists and formulas – you take notes during talks, you underline when you read and you already practise a rigorous spiritual regimen – before you dutifully lengthen your list of spiritual duties, back off. Do you really need more habits, or could it be that you simply need to practise greater effectiveness with the ones you already have?

Too many believers wear spiritual discipline like a straitjacket. They allow themselves to get sucked into a long, arduous list of requirements that serve only to squeeze the vitality, spontaneity and adventure out of faith and life. For these people Christ no longer brings freedom, and religion becomes a heavy burden. Most people can't live that way for long.

List lovers, remember the advice Galatians 5:1 offers: 'It is for freedom that Christ has set us free. Stand firm, then, and do not let yourselves be burdened again by a yoke of slavery.'

## Caution 2: Don't let the decision be negotiable

The second warning is for those who make the opposite but equally damaging error. They think, 'I don't need any structure or rigorous habits to make my heart grow. I'll just play it by ear and go with the spiritual flow. You know, "let go and let God" and wait to see what happens.'

At best this attitude is naïve; at worst it is self-deceived. Christ-followers cannot grow without structure and a sense of intentionality about their spiritual life, any more than people can lower their body fat or develop solid muscle tone by sitting back and eating sweets.

If a goal is really important to me, I discipline myself in order to achieve it. I decide in advance that practising to meet the goal is non-negotiable. Otherwise I can count on the fact that I'll bail out along the way. For example, one of my big goals is to stay healthy. With my genetic endowment, I would be insane not to exercise faithfully every day. So I have made a decision: I will jog, and my jogging time is non-negotiable.

I don't wait to jog until I feel like running. Let's be honest – how many days a week do I really want to do it? Not today, that's for sure! I need to stay at work longer. My biorhythms aren't right. It's a little chilly outside. It's going to rain. It's too sunny. My shoes are too tight. My knees ache. My couch looks inviting. The list is endless.

The same is true with prayer. When we get serious about learning to pray, it's time to make a decision: I will learn what disciplines are necessary to fuel my prayer life, and I will practise these disciplines regularly, without fail.

Maintaining good prayer habits is non-negotiable. I know that no discipline will, in and of itself, create a relationship between God and me. At the same time I know that I will not develop a rich, rewarding prayer life if I try to do it on the fly.

## Ask an expert

To learn the heart-building habits of prayer – the practices that expand our freedom and give us spiritual wings – we need look no further than the world's greatest expert on the subject, Jesus Christ himself. In all of history no-one has ever understood prayer better than Jesus. No-one has ever believed more strongly in the power of prayer, and no-one has ever prayed with as much fervour and frequency as he did.

His disciples recognized his expertise. Once, they stumbled upon Jesus praying privately and were so moved by his earnestness and intensity that when he finally got up from his knees, one of them timidly asked, 'Would you teach us to pray?' (see Luke 11:1).

Do you think they overheard him using complex theological terms that they wanted to learn? Or was it his dramatic motions and gestures or special effects – some paranormal set of activities – that they wanted to pick up?

I don't think so. I think they watched Jesus pray and could tell even from a distance that there was a depth of fellowship happening between Jesus and his Father that the disciples had never experienced before. There was a spiritual community between Jesus and the heavenly Father so rich and so real that the disciples couldn't help but say, 'We don't relate to the Father that way. Help us to do that.'

Some years ago I took five men on a sailing trip. We were out on the high seas for a week, and the night before we left to fly home, we had dinner at a local restaurant. All six of us were sitting around a table, and at the table next to ours sat a woman and a man, holding hands across the candlelit table and talking quietly as they gazed into each other's eyes. It was obvious that they were very much in love.

One by one, the men around our table noticed what was going on with that couple. And one by one, they excused themselves, saying, 'I think I'm going to go and call my wife.'

Motivating these phone calls was the vivid picture they saw of deep, satisfying, love-filled relating patterns. Which, in turn, made the men want to call their spouses. It's exactly the kind of thing that happened the day the followers of Jesus watched him praying. They saw something in the way Jesus related to his Father, and they immediately wanted it for themselves.

'Jesus, teach us,' they said. Why? Because they knew that in comparison to their Master, they were beginners in the school of prayer.

## Jesus' prayer principles

Hearing the disciples' plea, Jesus seized the teachable moment before him. This is what he said:

> When you pray, do not be like the hypocrites, for they love to pray standing in the synagogues and on the street corners to be seen by men . . . When you pray, go into your room, close the door and pray to your Father, who is unseen. Then your Father, who sees what is done in secret, will reward you. And when you pray, do not keep on babbling like pagans, for they think they will be heard because of their many words. Do not be like them, for your Father knows what you need before you ask him.
>
> This, then, is how you should pray:
> 'Our Father in heaven,
> hallowed be your name,
> your kingdom come,
> your will be done
> on earth as it is in heaven.
> Give us today our daily bread.
> Forgive us our debts,
> as we also have forgiven our debtors.
> And lead us not into temptation,
> but deliver us from the evil one.' (Matthew 6:5–13)

No other passage in Scripture reveals in such straightforward fashion how to pray:

- Pray regularly. Jesus said, 'When you pray . . .' not 'If you pray . . .'
- Pray privately. God is not impressed by public displays of piety.
- Pray sincerely. God is not interested in formulas. He wants to hear what is on our hearts.
- Pray specifically. Take the prayer we call the Lord's Prayer as a model.

And the best news of all is that the advice Jesus offered his disciples two thousand years ago applies to all of us still today.

# 5. PRAYING LIKE JESUS

Most Christ-followers I meet say they just don't have time for daily prayer. But it's always fascinating to discover what they do make time for. If they want to develop in any other area – piano, football, physical fitness – they diligently carve out time to practise. Take the America's Cup team from New Zealand. They practised intensively for two years, six days a week, eight hours a day, and they brought sailing manoeuvres to a level never achieved before.

My point is, people who are serious about something always make room for it in their schedules. If prayer is important to you, then you'll find time to do it. Truly, if we are to live in God's presence, we must shut out the world every once in a while so that we can hear God's voice and God's voice alone.

## Get away from distractions

If establishing a regular prayer time is important, so is designating a regular prayer place. Some people pray in public places, at social gatherings and at mealtimes just so they can be seen and heard and assumed to be religious. But prayer, Jesus says, is not a spectator sport. It is not something we are to engage in to give off signals of spirituality. 'Forget that idea!' says Jesus.

Instead, when you pray, go into your room and shut the door. Find a small room, an empty office, the workshop out in the garage, some secret place where you can be away from people and alone with God. That's where you can pray most effectively.

One man I know prays on his commuter train five mornings a week. 'The seat on that train is the place where I pray every day,' he says. 'I built my whole spiritual life in that seat and at that same time, each and every day.'

Before work, another friend of mine heads to the corner table of a local restaurant and prays there. A woman I know has a chair beside a sliding glass door overlooking her back garden, and that's where she prays every afternoon. Another sits at her computer desk in her office and prays before leaving work each evening.

The place you choose may be more important than you think. When you establish a time and a place, it becomes integrated into the rhythm of your life. I'm a morning person, so I typically arrive at work before anyone else is there. Every day, I sit down in my office chair, swivel around, prop my feet up and reach for my spiral notebook, a Bible and a weak cup of black coffee.

This routine has taken such root in my life that it tends to take precedence even over more logical considerations, such as whether I need to be in the office on a particular day. If I'm not preaching that weekend, or if it's my day off, most of the time I still show up, just to spend those precious moments with God.

But why the emphasis on privacy? Why shut the door?

First, there is an obvious practical reason. A private place ensures a minimum of distractions, and most people find distractions deadly when it comes to making connection with God. Almost any kind of noise – voices, music, a ringing phone, children, dogs, birds – can cause me to lose my concentration during a time of prayer. Even a ticking clock can catch me up in its rhythm until I'm tapping my foot and singing a country song to its beat.

Jesus knows how our minds are put together and surely would counsel, 'Don't bother fighting distractions, because you'll lose. Avoid them. Find a quiet place where you can pray without interruption.'

The practical reasons for privacy are important, but I think there is also a more subtle wisdom in Jesus' advice to pray in a secret place. Once you identify such a place and begin to use it regularly, a kind of aura surrounds it. Your prayer room, even if it is a laundry room in the basement, becomes to you what the Garden of Gethsemane became to Jesus – a holy place, the place where God meets with you.

## Create a special atmosphere

Some married couples have a favourite restaurant where they go for important nights out. They love the atmosphere. They find it easy to talk in that environment and they look forward to going there. It is a special place for their relationship. Some families have a regular holiday spot that feels almost like a second home to them. Great things happen to the family there and important memories are created.

In a similar way, when you create a secret place where you can really pray, over time you will look forward to going there. You will begin to appreciate the familiar surroundings, sights and smells. You will grow to love the aura of the place where you freely converse with God.

If you want to learn how to pray, find yourself a quiet place free of distractions. It doesn't have to be a chapel. It can be the utility room, the barn, your office or the front seat of your truck, so long as the surroundings are familiar and quiet.

Go there during the best part of your day – in the morning if you're a lark, late at night if you're an owl, or whatever time you feel most alert. The point is, commit to meeting with the Lord there regularly and with great anticipation for what he will do in and through you as a result of your consistency.

## Mean what we say

Not only did Jesus tell his disciples to pray secretly; he also told them to pray sincerely. 'Don't keep on babbling,' I imagine him saying. 'Be careful of clichés. Don't fall into the habit of using meaningless repetition.'

How easy it is to use sanctified jargon while praying! Certain phrases sound so appropriate, so spiritual, so pious that many people learn to string them together and call that prayer. They may not even think about the implications of what they are saying. For example, I sometimes hear a mature Christian say earnestly, 'Dear Lord, please be with me as I go on this new job interview,' or 'Please be with me as I go on this trip.' When you first hear it, the request sounds holy. Unfortunately it doesn't make sense. I'm often tempted to ask the one who is praying, 'Why do you ask God to do what he is already doing?'

In Matthew 28:20, Jesus says, 'Surely I am with you always, to the very end of the age.' In Hebrews 13:5, God says, 'Never will I leave you; never will I forsake you.' Jesus tells his disciples in John 14:18, 'I will not leave you as orphans; I will come to you.' One of Jesus' names, Immanuel, means 'God with us'. We don't need to ask God to be with us if we are members of his family. Instead we need to pray that we will be aware of his presence, that we will be confident because of it. Asking God to be with us when he is already there is one kind of 'babbling'.

Another kind of meaningless repetition is often heard at the dinner table. A person sits down to a meal that is a nutritional nightmare. The grease is bubbling, the salt is glistening, the sugared drink stands ready to slosh the stuff down. 'Dear Lord,' the person prays, 'bless this food to the nourishment of our bodies and grant us strength from it so that we may do your will.'

In fact, God's will might be for the person to say 'Amen', push back from the table and give the meal to the dog. Except that dogs matter to God too.

The apostle Paul tells us in 1 Corinthians 6:20 that God's will is for us to honour him with our bodies. Last time I checked, that includes putting the right things into your body. Don't ask God to bless junk food and miraculously transform it so that it has nutritional value. Doing that is acting like the schoolchild who, after taking a geography test, prayed, 'Dear God, please make Detroit the capital of Michigan.'

That's not how God works.

## Pray from the heart

God doesn't want us to pile up impressive phrases. He doesn't want us to use words without thinking about their meaning. He wants us simply to talk to him as to a friend or father – authentically, reverently, personally, earnestly. I heard a man do this once when I least expected it.

I attended a conference where a group of high-level Christian leaders were present. The conversation was intense; I had to strain to keep up with the theological and philosophical issues being discussed. Lunchtime came and we all gathered at a nearby restaurant called the Hole in the Wall. A seminary professor was asked to pray. As we bowed our heads, I felt sure the prayer would come out like some theology class dissertation.

The theologian began to pray. 'Father, I love being alive today. And I love sitting down with brothers in the Hole in the Wall, eating good food and talking about kingdom business. I know you're at this table, and I'm glad. I want to tell you in front of these brothers that I love you, and I'll do anything for you that you ask me to do.'

He went on talking like that for another minute or two. When he said 'Amen', I thought, 'I have some growing to do.' His sincere prayer showed me how often I pray on automatic pilot. But God isn't interested in stock phrases. Psalm 62:8 says, 'Pour out your hearts to him.' Talk to him. Say, 'Lord, this is how I feel today. I've been thinking about this recently. I'm worried about this. I'm depressed about that. I'm happy about this.' Talk to the Father sincerely.

#6

## Pray specifically

Besides praying privately and sincerely, Jesus counselled his disciples to pray specifically. He showed them what he meant by giving them a model prayer, the prayer we have come to call the Lord's Prayer.

Jesus' prayer begins with the words 'Our Father'. Never forget that if you are God's child through Jesus Christ, you are praying to a Father who couldn't love you more than he already does.

The next phrase, 'who art in heaven', is a reminder that God is sovereign, majestic and omnipotent. Nothing is too difficult for him. He is the Mountain Mover; he is bigger than any problem you could bring to him. Fix your eyes on his ability, not on your own worth.

'Hallowed be thy name.' Don't let your prayers turn into a wish list for Santa Claus. Worship God and praise him when you come to him in prayer.

'Thy kingdom come, thy will be done, on earth as it is in heaven.' Submit your will to God's. Put his will first in your life – in your marriage, family, career, ministry, money, body, relationships, church.

'Give us this day our daily bread.' The apostle Paul wrote, 'In everything, by prayer and petition, with thanksgiving, present your requests to God' (Philippians 4:6). Lay out all your concerns, whether big or small. If you need a miracle, ask for it without shrinking back.

'Forgive us our trespasses, as we forgive those who trespass against us.' Be sure you're not the obstacle. Confess your sins, receive forgiveness and begin to grow. Live with a forgiving spirit towards others.

'Lead us not into temptation, but deliver us from evil.' Pray for protection from evil and victory over temptation.

'For thine is the kingdom, the power and the glory, for ever and ever.' End your prayer with more worship. Acknowledge that everything in heaven and earth is God's. Thank the Lord for caring about you and for making it possible for you to talk to him through prayer.

'Amen.' Let it be so.

God-honouring prayers are not simply shopping lists. They are more than cries for help, strength, mercy and miracles. Authentic prayer should include worship: 'Our Father in heaven, hallowed be your name' (Matthew 6:9). It should include submission: 'Your will be done on earth as it is in heaven' (v. 10). Requests are certainly appropriate: 'Give us today our daily bread' (v. 11), as are confessions:

'Forgive us our debts, as we also have forgiven our debtors' (v. 12).

The Lord's Prayer is an excellent model, but it was never intended to be a magical incantation to get God's attention. Jesus didn't give this prayer as a paragraph to be recited; in fact, he had just warned against using repetitious phrases. Instead he gave it as a pattern to suggest the variety of elements that should be included when we pray.

## Reflect on your time with God

The trouble with magical incantations is that they are mindless. Too often we go through life without assessing what we're doing and what it all means. If we approach prayer this way, we simply can't expect any fruit to be borne.

Every year, the Willow Creek Association hosts more than one hundred thousand ministry and marketplace leaders at a conference called The Leadership Summit. I'm always amazed by how much effort gets poured into organizing speakers, planning programmatic elements, filming introductory videos, crafting promotional pieces and so forth. But equally intensive is the post-conference evaluation process. We invite more than a hundred pastors to a hotel in Chicago and spend a full day and a half peppering them with questions about why certain sessions worked or didn't work and why various songs or dances or dramas made an impact or fell flat. As a team, we decided a decade ago that we would never get better without stringent evaluation such as this.

Over the years, I've read many Christian authors who say that if Christ's followers aren't growing, it is because they are not making a habit of evaluating their lives. During various eras of my ministry, those authors were describing me to a T. I was moving fast, always on the go, but never going deep inside my own soul to see what was growing – or not growing – there.

I was neglecting to engage in the type of introspection real growth requires. And I was paying a hefty price as a result. I found myself committing the same stupid sins over and over again, living with the same heavy load of guilt.

I made the difficult decision that each day I would try honestly to assess my soul's condition. I would look inside myself and I would write down what I saw. Feeling awkward and embarrassed, I took out a spiral notebook and started to write. 'God, here are some frustrations in my life. They aren't going away, so I might as well take a look at them.' Or 'Here's a relationship I'm concerned about. It's not good, and I don't know how to improve it.' Or 'Here are some blessings you've poured into my life.' Then, after writing a paragraph or two, I would reflect on what I had written.

## Above all, pray!

It's been nearly twenty-five years since I started writing reflections about my day. Better able to concentrate, I soon began writing out my whole prayer and reading it back to God. Previously I'd get no further than 'Dear God' and I'd already be thinking of the person I was going to meet for lunch, or the board meeting agenda, or what my family members and I would be doing later that evening.

But when I began to move pen across paper, it became much easier to remain focused. It also forced specificity; broad generalities don't look good on paper. What's more, the practice helps to highlight precisely when and how God answers prayers. It's a discipline that has blessed my life in innumerable ways.

Still today, at the end of each month, I read over my prayer journal and see where God has moved in miraculous ways.

Whenever my faith falters, I flip open my journal and look for evidence that God is answering my prayers. I always find it. And if I can list a number of answers to specific prayers in January, I feel better prepared to trust God in February.

I encourage you to experiment and see what works best for you. Try writing out your prayers once a week at first. If you find it helpful, do it more often. If it cramps your style (or your hand) and makes you uncomfortable, then find another means that is more effective for you. The key is to practise praying – and to practise praying regularly, privately, sincerely and specifically.

If there is one final piece of wisdom I have gleaned from God over the years regarding activating the miracle of prayer in our lives, it is this: just pray.

I can write about prayer, you can read about prayer and you can even lend this book to a friend to show that you are encouraging others to pray. But sooner or later you have to fall to your knees and just plain pray. Then, and only then, will you begin to operate in the vein of God's miracle-working ways.

# 6. A PATTERN FOR PRAYER

Suppose one day you decide you need to up the ante on your physical fitness. You get off the couch, hop in your car and head to a nearby health club to check things out. When you walk through the door, you are greeted by a staff member who agrees to walk you from station to station, showing you each piece of state-of-the-art equipment. At the end of the orientation he asks if you're ready to set up a fitness plan – a thought that makes you a little queasy.

Seeing your hesitation, the staff member tries to explain his rationale further: 'You need a routine in order to work every muscle group properly and consistently as well as to keep track of how many repetitions you complete at which weight and chart your progress over time. Basically it's the only way to avoid becoming unbalanced.'

You see, playing around is one thing; following an established regime is quite another. It's true with exercise equipment and it's true as well with prayer. But I get ahead of myself.

Looking around the fitness centre, you see lack of balance running amok. A behemoth with bulging deltoids walks out of the free weight area. Still wearing his back belt, he tries to take a few laps around the track but stumbles and gasps in hopeless resignation. Another man glides effortlessly around the track. Eyeing him, you calculate that he's doing seven-minute miles without an ounce of strain registering on his face. But from his upper body appearance, you would venture a guess that his wife has to open the pickle jars and lug in the logs to stock the fireplace.

Health club instructors know that without a carefully structured plan we're all likely to become unbalanced. That's because we all tend to do what we enjoy and ignore the difficult or distasteful or untried.

## A pattern for prayer

Developing prayer fitness is similar to developing physical fitness: we must follow a pattern in order to stay balanced. Without a routine, we inevitably fall into the 'Please God' trap: 'Please God, give me. Please God, help me. Please God, cover me. Please God, arrange this.'

Oh, occasionally we'll toss a few thanks heavenwards when we notice that God has allowed some good thing to come our way. Every once in a while, if we get caught with our hand in the cookie jar, we'll confess a momentary lapse of sound judgment. And now and then, if we're feeling really spiritual, we might even throw a little genuine worship into our prayers – but only in those rare 'holy' moments.

If I sound sarcastic, it's because I know all about prayer that lacks balance. Unfortunately I'm a real pro in that department. And I can tell you from personal experience where out-of-balance prayer leads. Sensing the carelessness and one-sidedness of our prayers, we start to feel guilty about praying.

Guilt leads to faint-heartedness and that in turn leads to prayerlessness. See the cycle? Out-of-balance praying leads to no praying at all!

If you've seen this devastating trend unfold in your own life, then it's time to set up a prayer routine. The pattern I offer in the pages that follow is certainly not the only pattern out there, perhaps not even the best long-term pattern to use, but it's a fantastic place to start. It's balanced and it's easy to use. All you have to remember is the word ACTS, an acrostic whose four letters stand for adoration, confession, thanksgiving and supplication.

## Adoration: entering holy space

In my opinion it is essential to begin times of prayer in a posture of adoration. Let me give you four reasons why.

First, adoration sets the tone for the entire prayer. It reminds us whom we are addressing, whose presence we have entered and whose attention we have gained.

I've had countless experiences where I walk into a church somewhere in the world and am gripped for a moment in time. Something tells me that my feet are on holy ground and that I need to concentrate, to focus on what's going on around me. This is the sensation I try to replicate as I begin my prayer time with God. That initial pause – the acknowledgment of holy ground – somehow adds meaning to everything that follows.

One of the best ways I know for establishing this type of tone is to choose a psalm of praise and read or say it back to God. Two wonderful psalms of praise are Mary's song (the Magnificat), found in Luke 1:46–55, and Zechariah's song, found in Luke 1:68–79. And if you're so inclined on a particular day, why not sing God a song of your own?

Next, adoration reminds us of God's identity and inclination. As we list his attributes, lifting up his character and personality, we reinforce our understanding of who he is.

Often I begin my prayers by saying, 'I worship you for your omnipotence.' When I say that, I'm reminded that God is able to help me, no matter how difficult my problem seems to me. His power is enough.

I also worship him for his omniscience. No mystery confounds God; he will not have to scratch his head about anything I say.

I worship God for his omnipresence. Wherever I'm praying – in an aeroplane, in my car or on some remote island – I know he is present with me.

When facing major decisions, I may concentrate on his guidance. When suffering from feelings of inadequacy or guilt, I may praise him for his mercy. When in need, I may worship him for his providence or power.

We can praise God for being faithful, righteous, just, merciful, gracious, willing to provide, attentive and unchanging. When the spirit of adoration takes over and we begin pondering God's attributes, we soon say from the heart, 'I am praying to a tremendous God!' Which only motivates us to keep on praying.

Third, adoration purifies the one who is praying. When we have spent a few minutes praising God for who he is, our spirit is softened and our agenda changes. Those burning issues we were dying to bring to God's attention may seem less crucial. Our sense of desperation subsides as we focus on God's greatness, and we can truly say, 'I am enjoying you, God; it is well with my soul.' Adoration purges our spirit and prepares us to listen to God.

Finally, adoration is a worthwhile place to start because God is worthy of adoration. It should be hard to get past the 'Our Father' in our prayer without sinking in awe over that incredible miracle. 'How great is the love the Father has lavished on us, that we should be called children of God!' says 1 John 3:1. A God who is omnipotent, omniscient and omnipresent and yet who loves us, watches over us and gives us good gifts – this is an amazing God! Our heavenly Father is worthy of our worship, and so right at the beginning, let's commit to offering it to him.

Adoration is foreign to most people, and you will probably feel clumsy when you first try it. As with anything else you take up – a new sport, a new computer program, a new job – you have to stretch yourself and work at it to do it well. After a while, though, you progress in both comfort and proficiency. Adoration works the same way. And once it becomes a vital aspect of your prayer life, you'll find you can't get along without it.

## Confession: naming our faults

Confession is probably the most neglected area of personal prayer. We often hear people pray publicly, 'Lord, forgive us for our many sins,' and as a result, a lot of us carry that approach through to our private prayer lives. We throw all our sins onto a pile without so much as looking at them and we say, 'God, could you please take care of that whole dirty heap?'

This approach to confession is a colossal cop-out. When I lump all my sins together and confess them *en masse*, I neglect to feel the pain or embarrassment or shame that should be elicited in me. But if I take those sins out of the pile one by one and call each by name, it's a whole new ball game.

I determined a long time ago that in my prayers I would deal with sin specifically. I would say, 'I told So-and-so we had nine hundred people at the event, but I know there weren't more than five hundred there. That was a lie and therefore I am a liar. I plead for your forgiveness for being a liar.'

Or instead of admitting I had been less than the best husband, I would say, 'Today I wilfully determined to be self-centred, uncaring and insensitive. It was a calculated decision. I walked through the door thinking, "I'm not going to serve her tonight. I've had a hard day, and I deserve to have things my way." I need your forgiveness for the sin of selfishness.'

## Who's a sinner?

Many years ago I had an interesting conversation with a man who regularly attended our church. I had given a message on our sinfulness and our need for a Saviour. He came to my office and said, 'All this talk about sin is making me feel really bad. I, for one, do not consider myself a sinner.'

I could tell this was someone I could shoot straight with and so I said, 'Well, maybe you are and maybe you aren't. Are you up for a few questions? First up: you've been married for twenty-five years, right? Have you been 100% faithful to your wife for that entire time?'

He chuckled and said, 'Well, you know, I'm in sales. I travel a lot . . .' We both knew what he was admitting to.

'OK,' I said, 'how about this one: When you fill out your expense account, do you ever add something that wasn't strictly business?'

'Everybody does that,' he replied.

'Or, when you are out there selling your company's product, do you ever exaggerate the benefits – you know, say it will do something it won't or promise to ship it tomorrow when you know it won't go out until next Tuesday?'

'Hey, I didn't set the industry standard. That's just the way it's done!'

I looked straight at him and said, 'You have just told me that you are an adulterer, a cheat and a liar. Repeat those words after me – I am an adulterer, a cheat and a liar.'

He looked as if his eyes were going to pop out. 'Hold on a second,' he cried. 'I only said there was a little something on the side, a little this and a little that . . .'

'No,' I said. 'Just tell it like it is. You're an adulterer, a cheat and a liar. To me, that means you're a sinner in desperate need of a Saviour. And so am I.'

## The benefits of confession

When you have the courage to call your sins by their true names, several wonderful things fall into place. Your conscience will be cleansed. 'I finally said it,' you will think. 'I'm finally getting honest with God. I'm not playing games any more and it feels good.' You'll be flooded with relief that God has a forgiving nature, just as Psalm 103:12 promises: 'As far as the east is from the west, so far has he removed our transgressions from us.' And you'll finally feel free to pray for strength to forsake that sin from that point forward.

Frankly, we don't take confession seriously enough. If we did, our lives would be radically different. On about the fifth day in a row that you have to call yourself a liar, a greedy person, a manipulator or whatever term may be true for you, you say to yourself, 'I'm tired of admitting that. With God's power, I've got to root it out of my life.'

As God goes to work on your sins, you begin to see Paul's words from 2 Corinthians 5:17 being fulfilled in your life: 'If anyone is in Christ, he is a new creation; the old has gone, the new has come!'

## Thanksgiving: expressing gratitude

The T in ACTS stands for thanksgiving. Psalm 103:2 says, 'Praise the LORD, O my soul, and forget not all his benefits.' Paul writes in 1 Thessalonians 5:18, 'Give thanks in all circumstances, for this is God's will for you in Christ Jesus.'

This part of your prayer time requires you to make the simple distinction between feeling grateful and expressing thanks. The classic teaching on this comes from Luke 17:11–19, which tells the story of ten men whom Jesus healed of leprosy. How many of those men do you think felt tremendous gratitude as they walked away from Jesus after being completely healed of their incurable, disgusting, socially isolating disease? There's no question about it – all ten did. But how many came back, threw themselves at Jesus' feet and actually expressed it? Only one.

It's hard to miss Jesus' reaction. He is clearly disappointed by the nine who felt gratitude but didn't take the time to express it. And he is clearly satisfied by the one who came all the way back to say thanks.

If you're a parent, then you know exactly what I'm talking about here. You know how incredibly good it feels when one of your children spontaneously thanks you for something.

Last year I received a Father's Day card from Shauna, who is now in her thirties. It was very gracious, and she wrote some precious words about remembering things we did when she was little: my teaching her how to swim and windsurf and sail and ride a bike. Then she talked about her adolescent era. (Trust me, it was quite an era.)

But her key lines came at the end. She wrote,

> I know that little girls love to hear loving words from their fathers; but Dad, big girls need to hear them so much more. To know that you are proud of the life that I've chosen and the marriage and the vocation that I've chosen means more to me by a thousand than all those days of playing catch in the driveway. Your job as a father is so much more important in my life now than I ever imagined it would be. Thank you, Dad. I love you.

Talk about melting a dad's heart! But my point is this: God is our Father, and he, too, is moved when we express our thanksgiving.

I thank God every day for four kinds of blessings: answered prayers, spiritual blessings, relational blessings and material blessings. Almost everything in my life fits into one of those categories. By the time I've gone through each category, I'm ready to go back to adoration for all God has done for me, which is the perfect posture to have as one moves to the S in ACTS.

## Supplication: asking for help

Supplications are requests that you make of God. And truly, nothing is too big for God to handle or too small for him to be interested in. Still, I sometimes wonder if my requests are legitimate. So I'm honest with God. I say, 'Lord, I don't know if I have the right to ask for this. I don't know how I should pray about it. But I hand it over to you now, and if you'll tell me how to pray, I'll pray your way.'

I believe God honours that kind of prayer. James says, 'If any of you lacks wisdom, he should ask God, who gives generously to all without finding fault, and it will be given to him' (James 1:5).

At other times, when I think I know how to pray about a matter, I say, 'God, this is my heart on the matter, and I'd really like you to do this. But if you have other plans, far be it from me to get in the way. You've asked me to make my requests known and that's what I'm doing. But if what I'm asking for isn't a good gift, if the time isn't right or if I'm not ready to receive it, then I defer to your plan. Your ways are higher than my ways, and your thoughts are higher than my thoughts. If you have different plans, I want to go your way.'

It may help you to break your requests down into categories, such as ministry, people, family life and personal needs. Those are the ones I use, and here's how I pray accordingly:

Under ministry, I pray for Willow's church staff, our construction programmes, our weekend services and all the various ministries of our church. I pray that through our work God will draw people to himself by confronting them with the living Christ and rescuing them from the emptiness and alienation that comes from living a godless life.

Under people, I pray for Christian brothers and sisters in leadership positions, our elders, our board of directors and people I know who are struggling with physical disease. I also pray for those in my circle of friends who are living far from God, that God will draw them to himself.

Under family, I pray for my marriage, for my children and for my grandson. I ask God to make me a godly husband and father and grandfather. I ask him for help with decisions about finances, education, holiday time, you name it.

Under personal, I pray about my character. I say, 'God, I want to be more righteous. Whatever you have to bring into my life to transform my character, bring it on. I want to be conformed to the image of Christ.'

Break up your requests into whatever categories suit your purposes and then keep a list of what you've prayed about. After a few weeks, go back and re-read your list. Find out what God has already done. I think you'll be amazed by his faithfulness.

## ACTS and written prayers

I've found the ACTS formula especially helpful when I write out my prayers. Starting with adoration, I might write something like this: 'Good morning, Lord! I feel free to praise you today, and I'm choosing this moment when I'm fresh and ready, willing and able to get going, to stop and say that I love you. You are a wonderful God. Your personality and character bring me to my knees. You are holy, just, righteous, gracious, merciful, fair, tender, loving, fatherly and forgiving. I'm thrilled to be in a relationship with you today and I worship you now.'

After adoration I move to confession. I might write: 'Please forgive me for committing the sin of partiality. It is so much easier for me to direct my love and attention towards those who seem to have it all together. Without even realizing it, I find myself avoiding troubled people. I'm sorry. Thanks for your impartiality to me. Please forgive me, and now I claim your forgiveness.' Then I take my pen and cross out the sins I've written down, in effect saying, 'I thank you that I'm free from this. I'm glad the slate is clean. Thank you for forgiving me.'

Thanksgiving is easy for me. I thank God for specific answers to prayer, for helping me in my work, for people's responsiveness, for protecting our elders, staff and board, for material and relational blessings and for anything else that makes me particularly happy. Thanking the Lord every day keeps me from being covetous, and putting my thanks on paper reminds me of the incredible number of blessings I enjoy.

I'm glad supplication is last. Once I've worshipped God, confessed my sins and given thanks, it's OK for me to take out my shopping list. In fact, James 4:2 says, 'You do not have, because you do not ask God.' I used to be vague about what I needed. Along the way I uttered the sentiment 'Please help me and cover me and keep me out of trouble' more than a few times, but I don't do that any more. Now I list specific requests, leave them with God and regularly review them to see how he has chosen to answer them.

When I get up from praying, I feel as if a ton of bricks has been lifted off my shoulders. It says in 1 Peter 5:7, 'Cast all your anxiety on him because he cares for you,' and when I pray, I'm not just telling God my problems, but rather I'm turning over my biggest concerns to him. It's only when I've put them in his capable hands that I can go about my day in his strength and freedom.

## Getting started

Can I give you two straightforward ways to get your prayer routine started? Try the first one today and the second one tomorrow, and see which approach fits you better.

During your time with God today, write down your prayers. Take a sheet of paper and draw three horizontal lines across it, dividing it into four sections. Label the sections A, C, T and S.

In the first section, write a paragraph of adoration. List God's characteristics that especially move you today.

In the second, write a paragraph of confession. Specifically identify the sins that are on your conscience. (Feel free to torch the paper after your prayer time is up!)

In the third section, list God's blessings you're most thankful for.

And in the fourth, list your requests, whatever they may be.

Then, tomorrow, try saying your prayer out loud. Turn to page 203, 'A guide for private or group prayer', which you can use for your private devotions or for group prayer. Follow the prayer suggestions, reading the Scripture verses aloud and adding your own prayers as prompted.

Frame your prayers with the four ACTS categories – adoration, confession, thanksgiving and supplication – and see if the blessing of balance doesn't surface in your prayer life.

# 7. MOUNTAIN-MOVING PRAYER

Jesus said, 'I tell you the truth, if you have faith and do not doubt . . . you can say to this mountain, "Go, throw yourself into the sea," and it will be done. If you believe, you will receive whatever you ask for in prayer' (Matthew 21:21–22).

Jesus, of course, was not in the excavation business. He had little interest in relocating piles of rocks to the ocean's depths. He was using the term 'mountain' figuratively, in the hope of conveying to all believers that we can be confident that our prayers carry great power.

Our prayers can be more than empty wishes, vain hopes or feeble aspirations – but only when they are prayed from faith-filled hearts.

These are the prayers that move mountains. 'Whatever mountain stands in your path, whatever obstacle blocks your way, whatever difficulty immobilizes you,' Jesus might say, 'the prayer of faith can literally take it out of your life's equation.'

Sounds great, doesn't it? But how do we actually get this type of faith-filled life?

## Don't focus on the mountain

There are two main principles I've picked up over the years as they pertain to cultivating the type of faith that moves mountains. The first is this: Faith comes by looking at God, not at the mountain.

Some years ago a member of our church's vocal team and I were invited by a Christian leader to go to southern India. There we would join a ministry team of people from various parts of the United States. We were told that God would use us to reach Muslims and Hindus and non-religious people for Christ, and although we had no idea what to expect, we all felt called by God to go and consequently jumped at the opportunity.

When we arrived, the Indian leader met us and invited us to his home. Over the next few days, he explained that his father, a dynamic leader and speaker, had started the mission in a Hindu-dominated area. One day a Hindu leader came to his father and asked for prayer. Eager to pray with him, and hoping he would lead him to Christ, he took his Hindu guest into a private room, knelt down with him, closed his eyes and began to pray. While he was praying, the Hindu man reached into his robe, pulled out a knife and stabbed the man repeatedly.

My new friend, hearing his father's screams, rushed inside to help him. He held him in his arms as blood poured onto the floor of the hut. Three days later his father died. On his deathbed he said to his son, 'Please tell that man that he is forgiven. Care for your mother, son, and carry on this ministry. Do whatever it takes to point people towards faith in Christ.'

With more courage and faith than most people could even

dream of mustering, this man complied with his father's wishes. For over twenty years, he has been working with unwavering passion and intensity, starting more than one hundred churches and a medical clinic, along with many other kinds of ministries.

Every spring he rents a huge park, sets up a stage and a makeshift sound system, puts together some lights with bare wire and holds evangelistic meetings for a week. He advertises with posters and through loudspeaker announcements all around town, and as a result people come by the thousands and sit on the ground in front of the stage, men on one side and women and children on the other.

The evening meetings start at six o'clock. For about half an hour, they listen to recorded instrumental music, followed by a couple of special musical numbers. Then comes the warm-up sermon. Instructional, practical and relevant to everyday life, its simple objective is to show the listeners that Christianity makes sense.

At eight o'clock there are two more musical numbers, followed by the main message. It is always centred on the person of Jesus Christ – who he was, what he did, how he died, how his death pays the price for sin and how his resurrection gives power to people who put their trust in him.

From nine until nine-thirty, listeners – whether Hindu, Muslim or non-religious – are invited to put their faith in Christ. They are asked to come forward to receive forgiveness, cleansing and eternal life and then are challenged to abandon whatever other god or religious system they brought with them to the meeting and to put their faith solely in Jesus.

## A terrifying assignment in India

From Tuesday to Thursday during my week in this village, I had manageable assignments. Either I spoke at a much smaller morning meeting or I gave the warm-up sermon in the evening. But when Friday came around, the leader of the ministry said, 'Bill, I received a prompting from God, and I want you to give the main message tonight.' (I sort of wondered why I hadn't received a similar prompting, but I heard the man out.)

As he talked, I mentally pictured all the roadblocks I would face if I said yes. The language barrier would be almost insurmountable, even with a translator. I wasn't familiar with the culture, so I couldn't speak relevantly to the people's situations. I would have a hard time with humour. Not to mention, when was I supposed to prepare? The meeting was that night!

He left me alone for a few minutes to think and pray. But there were so many unknowns that every time I tried to pray about my decision, I'd get thirty seconds in and would be stymied by doubt and fear. 'What's the use? This just isn't the right opportunity for me.'

Evening fell and the man and I took a rickshaw to the park. As we approached, we could hear the first message over the loudspeakers, which meant I had a few more minutes to nurse my paranoia.

We took our seats at the back of the stage, and as I looked out over the crowd, I realized it was one of the largest sea of faces I had ever seen in my life. One of the Indian leaders poked me with his elbow and said, 'Twenty thousand here tonight, maybe thirty.' With that, any nugget of confidence I may have had fled in a hurry.

'This is going to be a disaster!' I thought. 'What am I doing here?' I looked behind the stage and saw the leader of the ministry and several of his trusted associates on their faces in the dirt, praying. 'I know what they're praying about,' I thought. 'They realize that this American who is going to give the main message is perfectly capable of emptying out the whole park in a matter of minutes.'

Each of those praying men lived in poverty and fought unbelievable odds on a daily basis in order to tell people of God's grace and love and forgiveness. They had given their whole lives so that people caught up in false religious systems could come to know the truth of Jesus Christ. And since these annual meetings were the focal point of their whole year's efforts, I felt sick at the thought of the setback their work would suffer because of my inept preaching.

## Great is thy faithfulness

The first speaker ended his message, which meant I had about ten minutes left before I'd be in the firing line. Moments later the vocalist from my church stepped up to the microphone to sing. 'I probably should support her in prayer,' I thought, 'but my turn is next, and when the chips are down, it's every man for himself.'

My praying took on new earnestness. 'O Lord, deliver me. Make it rain. Make me disappear. Make something happen here!' The mountain looked so tall and imposing that I saw no point in asking God to move it. I would be content if it would simply cave in on me and put me out of my misery.

As my pitiful prayers bounced around inside my doubt-filled mind, I faintly heard the vocalist.

Great is thy faithfulness, O God my Father,
There is no shadow of turning with thee;
Thou changest not, thy compassions they fail not;
As thou hast been thou forever wilt be.
Great is thy faithfulness! Great is thy faithfulness!
Morning by morning new mercies I see;

All I have needed thy hand hath provided –
Great is thy faithfulness, Lord, unto me!

Like me, our singer didn't know the language of her listeners. She couldn't just sing a song; it had to be heart-to-heart communication, or nothing worthwhile would happen. Little did she know as she communicated beautifully with the thousands of people sitting beyond the stage that she was also communicating with a faint-hearted, doubt-filled, faith-starved pastor who needed that song a lot more than the crowd did.

Something happened to me as I listened to the lyrics. 'Great is thy faithfulness . . .' As the words rolled through my mind, it suddenly dawned on me that all day long the focus of my attention had been on me – my language barrier, my cultural confusion, my inexperience, my weakness, my fear of failing, my terror of a crowd that size. I was looking squarely at my mountain, and all I could see was my inability to move it.

My prayers were futile because I was looking at my inadequacy instead of God's adequacy.

## A change of focus

As the song continued, I said to myself, 'My focus has got to change, here and now. How about looking at God, not at Hybels, for a few minutes!'

I didn't have much time, but I started saying intensely, 'I'm praying to the Creator of the world, the King of the universe, the all-powerful, all-knowing, all-faithful God. I'm praying to the God who made the mountains and who can move them if necessary. I'm praying to the God who has always been faithful to me, who has never let me down no matter how frightened I was or how difficult the situation looked. I'm praying to a God who wants to bear fruit through me, and I am going to trust that he is going to use me tonight. Not because of who I am, but because of who he is. He is faithful.'

By the time the song ended, I was a different person inside. I still would have taken a rain check if one had been offered, but at least I wasn't panicky any more. I was willing to proceed because the one true and faithful God was the object of my full attention. When I walked up to the podium with my translator, I prayed a prayer that was a mountain-moving prayer, for the simple reason that it was firmly fixed on God's adequacy, not my inadequacy.

I spoke with Spirit-given confidence that night – confidence based solely on God's sufficiency. I told the people who had gathered there that someone had shed his blood to pay for their sins. This someone was not a Buddha, not a Hindu god, not a character in a myth or a fairy tale. He was a real human being named Jesus, and he is God's only Son. I told them over and over again, 'You matter to him, my friends. He shed his blood for the forgiveness of your sin, so you could go free if you put your faith and trust in him.'

As I was speaking, I knew God was working. I ended the message and an invitation was given for people to trust Christ. I walked behind the stage, got down on my knees and started to pray: 'O Lord, I know how these people matter to you. Draw them to you now.'

Hundreds and hundreds of people came forward – Hindus, Muslims, unbelievers of all sizes and shapes, colours and ages. So many came that I thought my heart would burst. I was rejoicing for every single soul who found new life in Christ, and I was also rejoicing because that night, through prayer, God had taken a mountain called fear and cast it into the depths of the sea. That night I learned that God sees no barriers, even when I do. God is ready to use me. And when I focus on God instead of my mountain, he channels through me his grace and his power.

## Go through it

The second principle of mountain-moving faith is this: God gives us faith as we walk by his side.

As Joshua 3 opens, the Israelites are camped on the bank of the Jordan River. Forty years earlier, they had escaped miraculously from Egypt, but now, for an entire generation, they have been wandering in a rugged wilderness. So far all of their needs have been met miraculously by God, but now that they are within sight of the Promised Land, Canaan, they have an enormous problem: a river is directly in their path, and there's no convenient way around it. To make matters worse, it is flood season and any usual fording places are impassable. The waters are deep and turbulent and threatening.

True, God could easily make the river subside right before their eyes or toss a wide bridge across it. But he doesn't. Instead he gives Joshua a set of strange orders that he then passes on to the rest of the camp.

First, camp officers are to order the people to keep an eye on the ark of the covenant. As soon as they see the priests carrying it, they are to fall in behind them.

Second, the whole lot of them are to expect something amazing to happen.

And third, the priests are to pick up the ark and go and stand in the river.

## Take that first step

This last piece of the command will take a bit of courage. Yes, the Lord said he would provide a dry path through the river, but the priests have never seen this happen before. They hadn't even been born when the Red Sea was parted.

Having spent their entire adult lives in the wilderness, the priests are not swimmers. In fact, this is probably the first river they have ever seen close up. Although the Jordan is not typically vast and raging like the Amazon or the Mississippi, it can be quite menacing during flood season. And with a few hundred thousand anxious Israelites at their heels, it will be hard for the priests to change their minds and turn around if the river keeps flowing.

In spite of the challenges they faced, the priests had faith enough to obey. Joshua 3:15–17 says,

> As soon as the priests who carried the ark reached the Jordan and their feet touched the water's edge, the water from upstream stopped flowing . . . The priests who carried the ark of the covenant of the LORD stood firm on dry ground in the middle of the Jordan, while all Israel passed by until the whole nation had completed the crossing on dry ground.

God didn't give the priests absolute proof or even overwhelming evidence that the waters would part. He did nothing until they put their feet in the water, taking the first step of commitment and obedience. Only then did he stop the flow of the river.

In the same way, mountain-moving faith will be given to us as we step out and follow God's direction.

## Move over, mountain

How do you pray a prayer so filled with faith that it can move a mountain? By shifting your focus from the size of your mountain to the sufficiency of the Mountain Mover and then stepping forward in obedience. As you walk with God, your faith will grow, your confidence will increase and your prayers will have real power.

While the children of Israel are perched on the edge of the Promised Land, twelve spies go out to survey it. Numbers 13 tells us that ten come back saying, 'You wouldn't believe the size of the cities, the armies, the giants! We'd better look somewhere else.' Two come back saying, 'The God who is faithful promised he would give us the land, so let's go in his strength.' Ten looked at the size of the mountain and fell back; only two looked at the sufficiency of the Mountain Mover and wanted to move forward.

Israel's warriors are standing on a hill overlooking a battlefield, and the Philistine champion Goliath swaggers out to frighten them. We read in 1 Samuel 17 that the warriors declare, 'We're not going down there to fight him. He's nine feet tall. Look at his armour! Look at his spear! I don't want that thing in my ribs.' The adolescent shepherd David comes out, surveys the field and says, 'Look at the size of our God. Let me go!'

Probably every human being alive is standing in the shadow of at least one mountain that just will not move: a destructive habit, a character flaw, an impossible marriage or work situation, a financial problem or a physical disability. I wonder, what is your immovable mountain? It could be that you have stood in its shadow for so long that you've actually grown accustomed to the darkness. Perhaps you end every prayer on the matter by thinking, 'What's the use?'

I challenge you to shift the focus of your prayer. Don't spend a lot of time describing your mountain to the Lord. He knows what it is. Instead focus your attention on the Mountain Mover – the God who is full of glory, power and faithfulness. Then, following his leading, begin walking in faith. And watch your mountain step aside.

# GOD BREAKS DOWN THE BARRIERS BETWEEN US

# 8. THE HURT OF UNANSWERED PRAYER

Following nearly every weekend service, I'm approached by someone who asks for a little prayer clarification. 'Bill, didn't Jesus say that if we ask, it will be given to us, and if we seek, we'll find, and if we knock, all sorts of doors are going to get opened?'

These people aren't usually looking for a theological lesson. What they're typically trying to convey by alluding to Matthew 7:7–8 is that they've been asking, seeking and knocking . . . to no avail. I probe a little and then their frustration and confusion comes pouring out. 'I've been praying for my husband to stop drinking, and he came home drunk again last night.' Or 'I've been praying for a job, but no-one wants to hire a fifty-year-old middle manager.' Or 'I've been praying for my wife's depression to improve, and now she's threatening suicide.'

On and on the lamentations go, week after week, month after month, year after year. I couldn't begin to count how many people I've counselled about the mystery – and the agony – of unanswered prayer. And what's most puzzling is that the people who suffer most keenly are those who actually believe that prayer does move mountains!

In counselling sessions with people who are troubled because their prayers aren't being answered, I use a little outline I borrowed from a pastor friend of mine. It goes like this:

If the request is wrong, God says, 'No.' If the timing is wrong, God says, 'Slow.' If you are wrong, God says, 'Grow.' But if the request is right, the timing is right and you are right, God says, 'Go!'

We'll look at the first two problems – wrong requests and wrong timing – in this chapter, saving the third topic for chapter 9, where we can look at it in greater detail.

## Inappropriate requests

Some prayer requests, no matter how well intentioned, are just plain inappropriate. Jesus' disciples were not immune from making misguided requests. Not even the three who were closest to him – Peter, James and John.

These three once accompanied Jesus to the top of a high mountain. Suddenly God's full glory descended upon Jesus, and Moses and Elijah appeared beside him. Beholding God's splendour just a few feet from where they were standing, Peter, James and John dropped back in awe. Then Peter had a bright idea. In essence he said, 'Hey, Jesus, let's build shelters up here for you and Moses and Elijah. We'll be happy to stay on the mountain with you and just bask in your glory.'

Jesus' immediate response, in effect, was 'no': a thick cloud enveloped them, cutting off further conversation. Jesus and the disciples still had work to do down in the plains where people lived. They couldn't stay on the mountain top. Peter's request was inappropriate and therefore Jesus would not grant it. (See the complete story in Matthew 17:1–8; Mark 9:2–8; or Luke 9:28–36.)

Another time James and John came with their mother to Jesus, asking if they could reserve the best two seats in his kingdom for themselves. As if eternity were a French bistro or something. It wasn't merely a good view they were after; they wanted to be Jesus' guests of honour!

'Uhhh . . . no,' Jesus must have said. 'You don't even know what you're asking! There's going to be a lot of pain and hardship in my kingdom before my glory is revealed. Besides, the esteemed spots are already reserved.' In other words, 'Your request is inappropriate and I'm not going to grant it.' (For more, read Matthew 20:20–23 or Mark 10:35–40.)

James and John seem to have had a knack for requesting the wrong thing, because Luke 9:51–56 recounts yet a third time when they took this tack. Sometime after the transfiguration, Jesus and the disciples were denied passage through a Samaritan village. This setback irritated James and John so much that they asked Jesus to destroy the village with fire from heaven. Once again Jesus denied their request. In fact, he rebuked them for making it.

## Too loving to say 'yes'

If the disciples were capable of making wrong requests – requests that were self-serving, patently materialistic, short-sighted or immature – I feel sure that we are too. Fortunately God loves us too much to say 'yes' to inappropriate requests. He will answer such prayers, but he usually will say 'no'. I don't know about you, but I wouldn't want a God who would do anything else.

In hindsight I thank God for saying 'no' to prayers that at the time seemed appropriate. I remember once when my church was looking to fill a key leadership position. As a staff, we'd been praying for several years that God would show us the right person to fill the need. Then, simultaneously, we all thought of an individual who looked custom-designed to fill the slot. We asked God if this person was the one we were looking for, in faith agreeing to go ahead and contact him.

The elders commissioned me to meet with the person and ask him to consider joining our staff. We met at a nearby restaurant for lunch, and the whole time we were eating, I prayed, 'God, do I ask him about the role right now? Is this the time? We desperately need a person to lead in this area. Please tell me what to do.'

As I was ready to launch into my offer, it became apparent to me that God was saying, 'No. Don't ask him.' I had no idea why, but by God's grace I decided not to issue the invitation.

Towards the end of the lunch, the man said, 'Was there anything else you wanted to talk to me about?'

I answered, 'Not really. It's been great seeing you again.' And I went back and told the elders I couldn't present the ministry opportunity to the man.

Six months later we learned that there was deception in the life of that leader. His entire ministry crumbled around him, and still today he is disqualified from service. That could have happened while he was part of our congregation, and God could have been dishonoured in our midst. When I heard the tragic story, I silently prayed, 'Thank you, Jesus, for having enough love and concern for our body and for our elders and for our staff to just say "no".'

## The importance of motives

Most of us would never approach God with the intention of making a 'bad ask', but still, wrong requests float towards heaven all the time. The most famous wrong request is the one where we beg God to change the other person. Wives pray this about husbands, husbands about wives, parents about children, employees about bosses. In fact, whenever two or more Christian people have to relate closely to each other, somebody is bound to make this request.

Don't get me wrong; it's often perfectly fine to pray that someone will change. After all, that's what we do when we pray for conversions, for hearts to be softened and for bad habits or addictions to be broken. No, what I'm referring to are the times when we make requests that don't reflect authentic concern for the other person.

Whether we admit it or not, a lot of prayers probably sound to God like this: 'I don't want to face my own shortcomings. I don't want to work on this relationship. I don't want to change at all. Instead, why don't you just change the other person so that he will accommodate all my personal needs. Deal?'

If you pray that kind of prayer, my friend, God is likely to refuse.

## God's glory or mine?

There are plenty of other inappropriate, self-serving prayers masquerading as reasonable requests. 'Please give me this new account' may be a good request for account executives to make. There's nothing wrong in praying for help in business; we should bring all our concerns to God. But if our motivation is to show off in front of the other sellers, or to get rich in order to live lavishly, or to thumb our noses at supervisors who advised us not to go after the account, it's a wrong request and God is likely to say 'no'.

Or pastors may pray, 'O Lord, help our church grow.' Surely God would want to honour that request! But if a pastor's real meaning is 'I want to be a star with a big church, fancy programmes and lots of media coverage', the request is wrong.

Likewise, the Christian musicians who pray, 'Help my album sell and my concert tour to take shape,' could be asking for personal glory, no matter how often they refer to God on stage. We can fool ourselves into thinking selfish requests are appropriate, but we can't fool God. He knows when our motives are destructive, and he often protects us from them by saying 'no'.

Before bringing a request to the Lord, it's a good idea to ask: 'If God granted this request, would it bring glory to him? Would it advance his kingdom? Would it help people? Would it help me to grow spiritually?'

By forcing us to look closely at our requests, prayer purifies us. Then, if the purification process reveals that our motives were wrong, we can come before the presence of God once more and say, 'Lord, forgive me. Help me grow. Help me present requests that are totally in line with your will.'

If you've been praying diligently about a matter and have sensed resistance from heaven, I challenge you to review your request. You might just find your problem. Maybe your request is a cop-out on your part, an unwillingness to face the real issue. Maybe it is destructive in ways you don't understand. Maybe it is self-serving, short-sighted or too small. God may have something better in mind. Whatever the reason, if the request is wrong, God says, 'No!'

## The mystery of suffering

One further note on this subject before we move on: Sometimes the motivation behind our request is not wrong, but in the infinite mystery of things, the outcome still seems to be 'no'.

Several years ago a member of my men's small group

learned that he had a brain tumour. Each week for more than a year we gathered around him and prayed that God would spare his life, that God would touch his body with healing. We were very specific, not to mention completely pure in our motivations, as far as we knew.

We said, 'God, we're requesting a total healing, whether it comes through your direct intervention, through medical treatment, through surgery or through some other means. But until our friend's dying day, we will ask you to do a miracle because you've invited us to pray for what we really want to see happen. And more than anything else, this is what we really want to see happen.'

As I say, we prayed for healing this way for more than a year. And still our friend died. We learned the hard way that sometimes, for reasons we don't understand this side of heaven, God may choose to deny a healing.

Each day, all across the globe, Christ-followers come to this realization. Godly people are stricken with dreaded deadly diseases. Praying parents die without having seen their wayward children return to the fold. Unspeakable tragedies afflict believers and non-believers alike. The righteous suffer and the innocent perish.

As awful as these realities are, they're nothing new.

Luke 13:1–4 tells us that once a tower toppled onto eighteen Jews – unsuspecting worshippers who were crushed indiscriminately. In Acts 12 we see the apostle James beheaded while Peter is miraculously delivered. The apostle Paul suffers all his life from a thorn in the flesh and finally dies under the axe of the Roman executioner.

Many Christians sense that God hears and empathizes with their prayers, but some requests remain unanswered. Why would a caring God deny valid requests from faithful believers?

It is critical to remember that, despite the victory God has achieved over Satan in the ministry and resurrection of Christ, not everything is submitted to God yet. The enemy is still active. His years are counted and his end is sure, but in the meantime he still remains the prince of this world, opposing the ways of God at every turn.

He causes much suffering, and he often seems to have the upper hand, but make no mistake: God will have the final say, and he will assert his universal sovereignty in salvation and judgment at Christ's second coming. Because of this ultimate victory, Christians have the assurance that those very prayers that remained unanswered in this life will receive spectacular vindication in eternity. Then, Revelation 21:4 promises, God 'will wipe every tear from their eyes. There will be no more death or mourning or crying or pain, for the old order of things has passed away.'

## Not yet

The second part of the outline was this: If the timing is wrong, God says, 'Slow.' Which, for most of us, feels equally as bad as getting a 'no'.

We live in an instant society, always trying to do everything faster. Motorways and supermarkets have fast lanes and express tills, movies and TV shows can come to us 'on demand' and we think our computers need upgrading if they make us wait five seconds. That explains why people have said to me, 'I don't know what to think. I've been praying for something for three days now, and God hasn't done a thing about it.'

Parents know that children rank the words 'not yet' as nearly the most awful in the English language, second only to the word 'no'. You're leaving on a five-hundred-mile trip in the car. You're fifteen miles from home and you slow down for some traffic lights. Voices from the back seat ask, 'Are we there yet?'

'Not yet,' you say, and the groans and complaints begin.

'My birthday's tomorrow. Can I open my presents tonight? It's close enough.'

'All the other girls wear make-up to school. Why can't I?'

'Will you teach me to drive?'

Children hate to hear the answer, 'Not yet.' And there's an impatient child in all of us, a child who wants God to meet every need, grant every request, move every mountain right now, if not before then. So, when our wise and loving heavenly Father deems it best to say, 'Not yet,' what is our mature adult response? 'But God, you don't understand. I need it right now. Not three years from now. Not three months from now. Not three days from now. Read my lips as I pray – I need this now!'

## Trusting the Father

God, however, is no more intimidated by childish demands for instant gratification than are wise parents. He simply shakes his head at our immaturity and says, 'Kick and scream if you must, but you can't have what you want yet. Trust me. I know what I'm doing. I have my reasons.'

Be wary of insisting that you know better than God about when a prayer request should be granted. God's delays are not necessarily denials. He always has reasons for his not yets.

Sometimes God delays in order to test our faith. Do we think of him as a celestial vending machine that we should kick if we don't get an instant response, or will we instead choose to relate to him as a loving Father who will give us what we need when we need it?

Sometimes God delays so that we can modify our requests. Over time we may see that the original request wasn't quite legitimate. As we understand the situation better, we may want to modify it to make it more in line with God's will.

Sometimes God delays so that we can develop character qualities such as endurance, trust, patience and submission – qualities that come only when we wait patiently and trust in his timing. A lot of spiritual gains come through pain, hurt, struggle, confusion and disappointment. If we had our way, though, how long would any of us put up with these character builders without asking God to remove them?

We may not be able to see the reasons for the delay, but that shouldn't come as a surprise. We'd do well to stamp God's words from Isaiah 55:8–9 on the inside of our eyelids: 'My thoughts are not your thoughts, neither are your ways my ways . . . As the heavens are higher than the earth, so are my ways higher than your ways and my thoughts than your thoughts.' We are the creatures; God is the Creator. Only he knows what timing is best.

Frequently I've wondered if God was saying, 'No,' only to find out later that he was saying, 'Not yet,' so that he could orchestrate a greater miracle than I had the faith to pray for in the beginning. When the results are in, God's wisdom is clear, and I am glad I waited patiently for it to be revealed.

## My own worst problem

There is a third reason why our prayers may not be answered. It is possible that something is wrong in our lives, that we have set up some barrier between ourselves and God.

Imagine you've been on a holiday for two or three weeks. You come back and discover that the person you hired to mow your lawn went to the hospital the day after you left and has been in traction ever since. Your lawn is about eight inches high, and you know your feeble bargain basement mower is not going to handle it.

Fortunately for you, your neighbour has an expensive ride-on mower that will cut anything, and he has often said to you, 'Look, if you ever get in a jam, you can use my mower.' You decide to take him up on his offer.

On the way to his house, as you're mentally rehearsing your request, your neighbour's dachshund waddles up and starts bothering your trouser legs. Now, you hate dachshunds, especially this one. It howls, it messes up your lawn and it snaps at you – which is exactly what it's doing right now. You can hardly put one foot in front of the other without getting bitten or tripped up.

Exasperated, you give the little fellow a swift kick. Then you look up and see your neighbour standing on his front doorstep, arms folded, looking straight at you.

Is it a good moment to ask for the lawn mower? Or is there something you need to clear up before asking for favours?

God repeatedly invites us to come to him with all our needs. He offers us free access to all his resources. But some of us have a few things we need to clear up before taking him up on his offer, which is what the next chapter is all about.

# 9. PRAYER BUSTERS

When you pray, why do you pray?

What is it that drives you to your knees and catalyses your prayer experiences? What gives you fervency to pray more and more?

As far as I'm concerned, the greatest prayer motivator in existence is answered prayer.

When I pray about a sermon and God answers by giving me insight from his Word, a way of organizing the material, an apt illustration or a sense of his power as I give the message, I'm motivated to pray about the next sermon I work on.

When I pray for someone who isn't walking with God, and one day the person calls me up and says, 'I'm a member of the family now – I've surrendered my life to Christ,' I'm motivated to continue praying for the other people on my list who are living far from God.

When I pray over a difficult decision and then get a sense

of God's leading, follow his direction and see in hindsight that I made the best possible choice, I'm motivated to pray about all the decisions that come my way.

And when I pray about a need that cannot be met by any human means, and God meets it through his miracle-working power, I'm motivated to get down on my knees and pray for all sorts of needs, whether personal, ministry-related or global.

## Me, a problem?

Although answered prayer can be a great motivator by making me feel like Moses on the mountain with his arms upraised, directing the battle through his prayers, by contrast my prayer life takes an abrupt nosedive when I see no results from my diligent efforts. Nothing is more demotivating than suffering through a string of unanswered prayers. You call heaven, and no-one seems to be home. The troops are getting massacred before your eyes, so you feel like lowering your arms in defeat and asking, 'What's the use?'

For each unanswered prayer, it's important to check out three possible hindrances. In the last chapter we looked at two major reasons why prayers go unanswered: the request may be inappropriate, or the timing may be off. If you're faced with a long list of unanswered prayers, however, you may want to pay special attention to the third category: there may be a problem in the life of the person who is praying. (That would be you.)

It's unlikely that all your requests are inappropriate. Likewise, it's unlikely that your timing is always off, even though sometimes you may forge ahead of God's preferred pace. Sometimes the most likely reason why you're not getting the answer you want is that your prayers are being blocked. Not by God, mind you, but by you.

When prayers go unanswered, most people want to know what's wrong with God. After all, it's a lot easier to blame God than to look in the mirror and say, 'Oh, maybe I'm the problem.' Of the thousands of people I've counselled about the mystery of unanswered prayer, only an astute handful of them have asked, 'Do you think I might be the obstacle to the miracle I'm praying for?'

I once asked a group of church leaders to list biblical reasons for unanswered prayer. Most of the reasons they put down were in this third category – problems in the life of the praying person, or prayer busters, as I call them.

## Everything but prayer

The most common cause of unanswered prayer is prayerlessness.

Have you ever decided to pray about something, added it to your prayer list, maybe even told a friend that you are praying about it, but then never actually committed the 'something' to prayer? You may have talked a good game, but you never actually got down on your knees and petitioned the King of the universe – the One who is willing and able to solve any problem, any time, according to his plan.

In that case, why isn't God answering your prayer? Because you haven't yet prayed purposefully, fervently and expectantly.

I come across people all the time who are addressing their lives' most pressing needs by going to counsellors, reading self-help books, claiming biblical promises, practising self-discipline, confiding in Christian friends, practising assertiveness or submission or self-denial or positive thinking, and yet still their needs are not being met.

My response is always the same: 'Look me in the eye and tell me – yes or no – if you've prayed about this fervently and regularly over an extended period of time.'

Usually they shift from one foot to another, look down and mumble, 'Well, uh, you know . . . um, not really.'

I understand all too well. Guess how. Unfortunately I joined the club whose motto is 'When all else fails, pray' a long time ago. And my membership still stands. Why pray when I can worry? Why pray when I can work myself to death trying to get what I need without help? Why pray when I can go without?

Oh, the lies we tell ourselves.

## Regular, earnest and persistent

When was the last time you prayed diligently over a period of time for your spouse, your parents or your children? Or for someone to come to know Christ? Or for peace in the war-torn parts of our world? Or that God's power would cause a revolution in your church? Or that God would put you to work for his glory?

In the early days of my ministry I travelled to Korea to visit the world's largest church. At that time, from eight o'clock every Friday night until seven o'clock the next morning, ten thousand people gathered in an auditorium and prayed that God would take the church's ministry by storm. Every Saturday, several thousand people went to a hilltop they called Prayer Mountain, sat in its many caves and prayed fervently that God would work in a supernatural way.

In those days the church had one hundred thousand members. Some people might have thought it was large enough, but its members had a vision. Ten prayer-filled years later, the church membership was up to half a million. Today there are over a million. (When we work, we work; when we pray, God works, right?)

I've heard it said that if you bring a thimble to God, he'll fill it. If you bring a bucket to God, he'll fill that. If you bring a five-hundred-gallon barrel to God, he'll fill that too. Are you expecting God to fill your needs? Are you asking him to do so – regularly, earnestly and persistently?

## Contaminated by cheating

The second reason for unanswered prayer is the most obvious. Unconfessed sin cuts off our communication with the Father. As Isaiah 59:2 says, 'Your iniquities have separated you from your God; your sins have hidden his face from you, so that he will not hear.' Years ago I raced motorcycles. A motorcycle is a rugged machine that can take incredible abuse, but its fuel has to be pure. At refuelling time I would pour the fuel through a filter or a handkerchief to be sure no contaminants would prevent the engine from running at its full potential. Any speck of dirt could cause a loss of power. Likewise, if you let even a little sin into your heart, it's going to contaminate your prayers. Your Christian life will not achieve its full potential.

God expects us to maintain strict personal integrity. He expects us to show thoughtfulness and love towards others and to maintain a relationship with him. Micah 6:8 paints a clear picture of God's expectations: 'What does the Lord require of you? To act justly and to love mercy and to walk humbly with your God.' If we refuse to do these things, we are presumptuous to expect God to answer our prayers.

If you're tolerating sin in your life, my friend, don't waste your breath praying unless it's a prayer of confession. Receive the Lord's forgiveness and then he will listen when you pour out your heart to him.

## Broken relationships

The third prayer buster is unresolved relational conflict. Matthew 5:23–24 says, 'If you are offering your gift at the altar and there remember that your brother has something against you, leave your gift there in front of the altar. First go and be reconciled to your brother; then come and offer your gift.'

This principle is extended in 1 Peter 3:7: 'Husbands . . . be considerate as you live with your wives, and treat them with respect as the weaker partner and as heirs with you of the gracious gift of life, so that nothing will hinder your prayers.'

Most of us grossly underestimate how committed God is to building and maintaining a loving community, a family. He adopts us into his family, and he wants us to carry our relationship with him into our relationships with others. If we do good to our brothers and sisters, it is like doing good to Jesus himself, says Matthew 25:31–46. Since God has forgiven us, Ephesians 4:32 and Colossians 3:13 affirm, we should forgive others.

There's no point in trying to pray if we are engaged in ongoing conflict with a family member, a co-worker, a neighbour or a friend. We read in 1 John 2:9, 'Anyone who claims to be in the light but hates his brother is still in the darkness.' God will listen when you come out into the light, confess the sins that drove you and the other person apart and attempt to mend the relationship.

Of course, it isn't always possible to make amends, but Romans 12:18 encourages us to try: 'If it is possible, as far as it depends on you, live at peace with everyone.' Sometimes the other person would rather continue the warfare than accept your apology. If this happens, look deep into your heart. Have you sincerely tried to restore the relationship, or are you holding something back? Do you really want restoration, or would you rather blame the other person and let the rupture continue?

If your attempts have been wholehearted and honest, God will not let the broken relationship stand in the way of your prayers. But if your reconciliation attempts have been half-hearted and self-serving, then try again – for real this time.

**Dear Santa Claus . . .**

Selfishness is the fourth prayer buster. James 4:3 puts it this way: 'When you ask, you do not receive, because you ask with wrong motives, that you may spend what you get on your pleasures.' Many of the inappropriate requests we looked at in the last chapter are wrong because they are selfish, and selfishness is an all-too-common barrier between the Christian and God.

How would you feel if your prayer requests were made public, displayed on a billboard or hoarding? 'Dear Lord, make me famous. Make me rich. Make sure I have a good time. Make all my dreams come true.'

We may never use those exact words, but our motives often convey this level of self-seeking nonetheless. When I began to study prayer, I was devastated over this point. I went over my usual prayers and had to face up to a lot of ugly covetousness. There was great confusion between wants and needs, rights and favours, justice and grace, and convenience and conformity to Christ.

I discovered that, in effect, I'd been pleading with God, 'Keep me from trial or tragedy or pain or anything that would make me really grow and become a man of God. Just give me a convenient, happy, satisfying, problem-free life.'

When Jesus prayed the model prayer we call the Lord's Prayer, his first requests were that God's name be shown reverence, that his kingdom come, that his will be done. Essentially the polar opposite of the self-centred, short-sighted prayers I'd been saying.

I'd been wondering why my prayers were infrequently

answered, but when I took a good look at what I'd been praying for, things became terribly clear. If God had granted my patently selfish requests along the way, I felt sure I would have been spiritually destroyed.

## Hearing the cry of the poor

The fifth prayer buster is uncaring attitudes. Proverbs 21:13 says, 'If you close your ear to the cry of the poor, you will cry out and not be heard' (NRSV).

A beautiful passage in the Old Testament tackles this prayer buster head-on. Isaiah 58:3 tells us that the Israelites were wondering why God was not answering their prayers. They had even fasted and humbled themselves – and still he did not listen. Here is what he told them through his prophet:

> On the day of your fasting,
>   you do as you please
> and exploit all your workers . . .
> You cannot fast as you do today
>   and expect your voice to be heard on high . . .
> Is not this the kind of fasting I have chosen:
> to loose the chains of injustice
>   and untie the cords of the yoke,
> to set the oppressed free
>   and break every yoke?
> Is it not to share your food with the hungry
>   and to provide the poor wanderer with shelter –
> when you see the naked, to clothe him,
>   and not to turn away from your own flesh and blood? . . .
> Then you will call, and the LORD will answer;
>   you will cry for help, and he will say: Here am I. (vv. 3–9)

God is committed to developing a people who will reflect his character in this world, and his character always expresses concern and compassion for the afflicted.

I once saw a cartoon picturing hundreds and hundreds of people lined up as far back as the eye can see. Each person was thinking the same thing: 'What can I do? I'm just one person.'

As 'just one person', you may not be able to change the world. You can, however, look for a small way to care. Perhaps your church works with a soup kitchen or prison ministry. Maybe your skills could make a small difference in today's evils of unemployment, illiteracy, child abuse, alcoholism or suicide. If your ear is open to the afflicted, God will keep his ear open to you. (For more on this idea now, skip ahead to chapter 16.)

### A God who is able

Inadequate faith is the final prayer buster. James 1:5–8 says,

> If any of you is lacking in wisdom, ask God, who gives to all generously and ungrudgingly, and it will be given to you. But ask in faith, never doubting, for the one who doubts is like a wave of the sea, driven and tossed by the wind; for the doubter, being double-minded and unstable in every way, must not expect to receive anything from the Lord. (NRSV)

Is God able? Is he omnipotent? If you don't own that doctrine, you might as well ditch prayer, because if your prayers have clouds of doubt hanging over them, they won't get past the ceiling. Before getting down on your knees, go to Scripture and look at what God has done for his people. Then review his track record in your own life, looking for evidence of his power, his faithfulness and his provision. Tune your mind properly so that when you finally do pray it will be to a God whom you are convinced is able.

The more you are convinced of God's ability, the more he demonstrates his ability to you. Jesus never tells his followers to throw wishes heavenwards. Instead he says, when you pray, plan on seeing a mighty demonstration of God's power.

**God says, 'Go!'**

If the truth were known, often you and I are the only obstacles standing in the way of our receiving a desperately needed miracle. Our requests may be right. The timing may not be a problem. But when our lives are wrong, God says, 'Before I grant your request, I want you to grow. Put that sin away. Change your attitude. Stop that practice; end that pattern; get off that merry-go-round; reconcile that relationship; soften up your spirit; repent and receive forgiveness.' In other words, he says, 'Grow!' And, as a result, 'I'll throw open the floodgates of heaven and pour out so much blessing that you will not have room enough for it!' (see Malachi 3:10).

Perhaps none of us truly understands how much God wants to change that impossible circumstance, touch that untouchable person or move that immovable mountain in our lives. But the truth is, we matter to him. And more than anything, he wants us to find him faithful to meet our needs and grant our requests, if only we will free him to do it.

Always remember, when our request is right, when the timing is right and when the person is right, God says, 'Go!' I believe nothing motivates people to develop their prayer lives more than answered prayers. And once the prayer busters are dealt with and dispatched, the way is clear for God to answer one prayer after another.

# 10. COOLING OFF ON PRAYER

A few months ago I was talking with some embarrassed Christians. They used to have a good prayer life, they told me. But things had changed. They no longer prayed as they once did, and they felt ashamed. One man described it like this:

'When I was a brand-new believer, the thought of talking with the God of the universe, the thought of God listening to me – caring about me, responding to my concerns – it was so overwhelming, I could barely take it in.

'Once I learned I could actually do this, I began to pray all day. I prayed when I got up. I prayed at the breakfast table. I prayed in the car on the way to work. I prayed at my desk, with friends over the telephone, at lunch, with my family at dinner, with my children when I put them to bed. I prayed with my small group. And I loved it when we prayed at church.

'I prayed all the time, and it brought me such joy! God was answering my prayers. My life was changing. Other people's lives were changing. It was wonderful!'

'So, what happened?' I asked.

'I don't know,' the man said. 'I honestly don't know. The whole thing just cooled off.' Then he said with great sadness, 'I don't pray much at all any more.'

## The prayerless season

I knew where this man was coming from. 'Almost every follower of Jesus Christ at some time has experienced exactly what you describe,' I said. 'I know I have.'

When I look back over the years of my spiritual life, I see certain seasons when I prayed eagerly and often. I was filled with joy and the anticipation of God's blessings. Supernatural things happened in my life, in the lives of people I prayed for and in the church.

And then, for who knows what reason, my prayer life would begin to wind down until I had almost given up on praying. I would still pray at meals and at church functions, of course, but would otherwise not engage. Prayer would seem dry, tedious and pointless. This prayerless season could last for weeks or even months.

Then suddenly God's power would flood into my life again, just as before. Once again I would delight in coming into God's presence. Once again I would pray often and with results.

That is, until the fade began again, as it always seemed to do.

What causes these ups and downs in our prayer life? Why do we lose interest in prayer? Why do we stop praying?

One reason why we stop praying or let our prayer lives fade is that we are too comfortable. When the storms rage and the winds howl and the waves break over the deck, everyone on board is praying like crazy. When the dreaded phone call comes in the middle of the night, when the doctor says it doesn't look good, or when your spouse says someone else is looking mighty attractive, prayer is almost second nature. In difficult situations like those, everyone prays – fervently, repeatedly, hopefully, even desperately.

And then the storm passes, the seas settle down, the wind diminishes and God proves himself faithful yet one more time. A big part of our motivation to pray subsides and the great prayer fade begins.

## Forgetting God

Understandably this prayerless pattern dramatically affects the heart of God. He is not beyond feeling used by his children. Especially when we act like students who phone home only when their money runs low.

There is a theme running through the Old Testament where God blesses his children, and they forget him. He blesses them again, and they forget him again. They get into big trouble and beg for help, and God comes through with an eleventh-hour rescue. Yet they forget him once again.

Read, for example, the sad litany in Psalm 78:41–42. Though God gave Israel the law, divided the sea so they could pass through, guided them through the desert, gave them miraculous food and water and drove back their enemies, 'again and again they put God to the test' and 'did not remember his power'. Or in Psalm 106:7–13, which says:

> When our fathers were in Egypt,
>   they gave no thought to your miracles;
> they did not remember your many kindnesses,
>   and they rebelled by the sea, the Red Sea.
> Yet he saved them for his name's sake,
>   to make his mighty power known.
> He rebuked the Red Sea, and it dried up;

he led them through the depths as through a desert.
He saved them from the hand of the foe;
from the hand of the enemy he redeemed them.
The waters covered their adversaries;
not one of them survived.
Then they believed his promises
and sang his praise.
But they soon forgot what he had done
and did not wait for his counsel.

The verse that precedes this passage says, 'We have sinned, even as our fathers did.'

Surely we don't want to forget God as well! Surely we want to stay mindful of God's goodness, and we want our prayer lives to be consistent.

Jesus assumed that his followers would make time for prayer. If we find we are praying less and less, it could be that we have never made prayer a fixed part of our everyday routine.

Some people have a prayer time even before they kick off the covers in the morning. Others pray over coffee or at lunch or right after work or school or after dinner or just before bedtime. The time of day we choose for prayer doesn't matter, as long as we keep it faithfully. Prayer must be part of the rhythm of our daily lives, as we looked at previously.

Choose a time when you are usually undisturbed, when you can shut the world out and tune in to God. At the same time, choose a place that can be your refuge, your sanctuary, while you are sitting in God's presence, as was noted in chapter 5.

## Old-fashioned sin

But say you have an established time and place to meet with God each day. What do you do when you just don't feel like going there any more? What do you do when you are no longer eager to pray?

When trying to help others understand why they don't pray any more, I often say, 'Let's go back. Do you know when you started feeling this way? What else was happening in your life at that time?'

People who are honest and self-aware often admit that perhaps guilt or shame is the cause for their prayerlessness: 'Well, you know, it was back when I was partying pretty heavily, and I started running around a lot and letting my life get out of control.'

Someone else will say, 'It was when things got really busy at work and greed got its hooks in me and making money started to be the driving force in my life.'

'I think it was when I was getting some counselling, and it was helping me at first. But then, instead of facing my problems, I got all absorbed in myself, and before you know it I became the centre of my universe. I pushed God off to the side.'

'It must have been back when I moved in with my boyfriend.'

I have to tell these people that, whatever the details, old-fashioned sin is more than strong enough to create an ever-widening gap in one's relationship with God. The wider the gap, the less likely we are to pray. And the less we pray, the wider the gap becomes.

People at Willow are quite aware of the fact that I don't like our dog. Or didn't like it, I should say. He's dead now. Which, if you ask me, is a good thing. But anyway, when he was not dead, I would come home from the church after a long, hard day and the dog would be all excited to see someone from the human race – until it noticed that it was me walking through the door.

Still, the dog would dart towards the laundry room because that's where the dog treats were stored and because this particular dog was a total con artist. It would spin circles all around that area of the house, trying its best to look cute so that I'd get the message: 'Give me a treat!'

Other family members would indulge the little thing, but not me. Not a chance. I'd stand firm and, in exchange for his aren't-I-cute look, would give him a look that said, 'Get real! You didn't work today, you lazy little hound! You don't get a treat for a ten-hour nap!'

It would then give me a look that said, 'OK, well, that didn't work so well,' and it would finally go away.

(To be perfectly honest, every once in a while, I would give the dog a treat. On those occasions it would almost audibly say, 'What are you doing?' To which I'd say, 'I'm playing mind games with you, that's what I'm doing.')

Sometimes I'd come home and the dog would be nowhere to be found. Which was always a bad omen. It always meant one of three things: furniture had been chewed, a lamp had been knocked over, or a little surprise had been left on our carpet. The worst sign, though, was when I'd walk through the door and the dog was lying underneath the coffee table with his tail between his legs and his back turned towards me. I'd think, 'Oh no. No question about it, that dog did something awful!'

You know how I'd know? Because *he* knew he'd done something awful. He wasn't trying to con me out of a treat by the door. Far from it! Instead his body language said, 'Clearly now is not a good time to ask Master Hybels for anything, so I am just going to lie low and make myself . . . scarce.'

Does this remind you of any Bible stories? Perhaps one from Genesis?

The Bible says that just after Adam and Eve disobeyed God in the Garden of Eden, they went and hid in the bushes. They lay low. They made themselves scarce. Which is, by the way, our human-nature tendency as well. I'm certainly not endorsing it, but I am acknowledging that, when we sin and resist God's promptings and violate his Word, it is difficult to motivate ourselves to have the same frequent, casual conversations with God that we did before our foul-up.

Most of the time we reason, 'I don't think it's a good time to ask God for anything. No, I think I'd better just lie low for a while and make myself scarce.'

## Despising God's name

I remember a time when I was colouring outside the lines. I knew I was sinning, but still I wondered why my early-morning prayer times at the office seemed cold and mechanical. I had a regular prayer time and a regular prayer place; for some reason, though, I just didn't want to get into a deep discussion with God.

Then I read God's words in the book of Malachi. '"Where is the respect due me?" says the LORD Almighty. "It is you, O priests, who despise my name." But you ask, "How have we despised your name?"' (1:6)

'In lots of ways,' God says through Malachi. 'Let me name a few.'

'You have been cheating God.' Despite God's clear instructions to offer only the best animals as sacrifices to the Lord, Israelites were taking their prize animals to market, where they could get top prices for them. Malachi 1 reveals that they then took the worthless animals – the blind, the lame, the ready to die – and brought them to God's altar.

'You have also been cheating the poor' – paying absurdly low wages, making life economically impossible for single mothers and treating illegal immigrants unjustly (Malachi 3:5).

'In addition, you have been cheating your families.' Divorce was rampant.

> You weep and wail because [the Lord] no longer pays attention to your offerings or accepts them with pleasure from your hands. You ask, 'Why?' It is because the LORD is acting as the witness between you and the wife of your youth, because you have broken faith with her, though she is your partner, the wife of your marriage covenant. (Malachi 2:13–14)

Through Malachi, God exclaimed, 'After cheating me, the oppressed among you and even your own families, you have the audacity to ask for my blessing? You blatantly sin against me and then have the gall to ask for favours? You rebel against me and then expect me not to be affected by your disobedience? Excuse me, but I am deeply impacted. Your sin breaks my heart. It feels like betrayal.'

Friend, if you and I do not live in submission to God, we lose the sense of warmth and closeness with him. We may feel nostalgic about the prayer times we used to have, but we've put up a sin barrier that will have to come down before we can enjoy a loving relationship with him again. We can have no deep, ongoing fellowship with God unless we obey him – totally.

## Pulling down the barrier

Astoundingly the Scriptures tell us that the God we have sinned against, the God we have shaken our fist at, holds out his arms to us and says, 'Come on back. You don't want to live that kind of life, do you? You don't want to go where that path leads. Admit your sin. Tell me you've fouled up. Agree with me that you're on the wrong track. Come on back, and we'll relate closely again. Then your prayers will be rich and real. We'll walk together once more.'

'Come now, let us reason together,' says the Lord in Isaiah 1:18. 'Though your sins are like scarlet, they shall be as white as snow; though they are red as crimson, they shall be like wool.'

If you have pumped your fist at God, the good news is that you can come back into fellowship with him right this minute. You can repent just by saying, 'God, I'm sorry for . . . Please forgive me. I want to turn from this, and I want to come back into relationship with you.'

When you pray that prayer, God will restore you. What's more, you'll pray a different kind of prayer after that because you will have been put back on track again.

## Is God deaf?

Perhaps you have made room for prayer in your daily schedule and you are unaware of any sin coming between you and God. All the same, you know you are drifting away from him. You are about to give up on prayer because you are discouraged, disillusioned or even despairing.

You prayed fervently that your dad would survive the surgery – but he didn't. You prayed that your son and daughter-in-law would reconcile and stay married – but they wouldn't. You prayed that your business would withstand a new competition – but it couldn't.

You know that your sins are confessed and you are trying to lead an ethical life. Your requests are not selfish. And now that your dad has died, your children are divorced or your business is defunct, God can't be telling you to wait. It's too late for that.

Apparently prayer just doesn't work, so why waste your

breath? If heaven doesn't listen, if God doesn't care, or if he lacks the power to change things, then why pray? Better to face reality and stop kidding yourself, right?

If you've had a crushing disappointment that prayer did not seem to fix, and if you're an honest Christ-follower, you have asked yourself questions such as these. While I do not have a pat answer for you – indeed, some things will never be clear this side of eternity – I can tell you what Jesus said to his disciples when they felt discouraged.

Remember the passage about the persistent widow from Luke 18? Jesus told his disciples – and us – that they should pray and never give up.

I plead with you, do not lose heart. Keep on praying, because the Father does listen. He hears every prayer we pray, and he cares deeply about everything that affects us. He has unlimited power to bring to bear on whatever is causing our concern. True, he doesn't answer every prayer the way we fallible humans wish he would. But he loves our company, he wants us to endure in prayerfulness and he is eager to do whatever is best for us.

## 'I kept on praying'

Some years ago we had a baptism Sunday when hundreds of people publicly affirmed their decision to follow Christ. It was incredible! Afterwards, on the stairs, I bumped into a woman who was crying. I couldn't understand how anyone could weep after such a celebration, so I stopped and asked her if she was all right.

'No,' she explained, 'I'm struggling. My mother was baptized today.'

'This is a problem?' I thought.

'I prayed for her every day for twenty years,' the woman said, and then she started crying again.

'You're going to have to help me understand this,' I said.

'I'm crying,' the woman replied, 'because I came so close – so close – to giving up on her. I mean, after five years, I said, "Who needs this? God isn't listening." After ten years, I said, "Why am I wasting my breath?" After fifteen years, I said, "This is absurd." After nineteen years, I said, "I'm just a fool." But even though my faith was weak, I kept praying. And finally she gave her life to Christ. And that woman was baptized today.'

Looking me dead in the eye, she said, 'I will never doubt the power of prayer again.'

# GOD SPEAKS TO OUR HEARTS

# 11. SLOWING DOWN TO PRAY

We've looked at several important aspects of prayer:

- God's gracious invitation for us to come to him as to a father.
- His incredible power to do more than we ever dream of asking.
- The habits and attitudes Jesus said we must cultivate in order to pray effectively.
- The categories we need to be sure to include in our prayers.
- The reasons why our prayers are not always answered in the way we wish.
- Some reasons why our prayer lives dry up from time to time.

This information about prayer is important, but it will do us no good if we never slow down long enough to pray.

And most of us are far too busy for our own spiritual good.

## Rev that engine

If we are involved in the marketplace, we are trained to believe that time is money. That's why we talk about managing time, using it efficiently and profitably and – as a result of our concern – dealing with time pressures. Cram more in. Start earlier. Work later. Take work home. Use a laptop on the train. Phone clients while you drive. Check your e-mail while you fly. Schedule breakfasts, lunches and dinners for profit. Performance, performance, performance – it's the key to promotion, to bonus increase and to power. Everyone knows this.

In car terms, an ordinary engine turns about four thousand revolutions per minute, or RPMs, and some racing motors can turn up to ten thousand. The marketplace mentality says, 'Rev it to ten thousand as soon as you get up in the morning, and keep it there until you collapse in the sack at night.'

Of course, getting caught up in that intense pace can be rewarding. It's exciting when the adrenalin starts to flow and you get on a roll, when your motor starts racing faster and faster. But you probably know as well as I do that it leaves precious little time for quiet moments with God.

You don't have to work outside the home to be overcommitted, either. Women with small children know what it means to do ten thousand RPMs all day long. Almost every minute of every day is consumed by those little creatures who pull on your trouser legs, colour on your walls, track mud on your carpet, throw food on your floor and then have the audacity to scream at the top of their lungs all night long.

The pace of working single parents is double or triple that of the rest of us. It is incomprehensible to me how they can meet the incessant demands of work all day and then go home to face the even more incessant demands of their children, with no time out in between.

I see pastors, elders and church board members operating at the same relentless pace as everyone else. Never a dull moment (and never a reflective moment either). With greater and greater frequency, I find myself asking, 'Where does the still, small voice of God fit into our hectic lives? When do we allow him to lead and guide and correct and affirm? And if this seldom or never happens, how can we lead authentic Christian lives?'

## The authentic Christian

Authentic Christianity is not learning a set of doctrines and then stepping in cadence with people all marching the same way. It is also not simply humanitarian service to the less fortunate. It is a walk – a supernatural walk with a living, dynamic, communicating God. The heart and soul of the Christian life is learning to hear God's voice and then developing the courage to do what he asks us to do.

Authentic Christians are persons who stand apart from others, even other Christians, as though listening to a different drummer. Their character seems deeper, their ideas fresher, their spirit softer, their courage greater, their leadership stronger, their concerns wider, their compassion more genuine and their convictions more concrete. They are joyful in spite of difficult circumstances and show wisdom beyond their years.

That's because authentic Christians have strong relationships with the Lord – relationships that are renewed every day. As the psalmist said of godly people,

> Their delight is in the law of the LORD,
> and on his law they meditate day and night.

> They are like trees
> planted by streams of water,
> which yield their fruit in its season,
> and their leaves do not wither. (Psalm 1:2–3 NRSV)

Embarrassingly few Christians ever reach this level of authenticity, because most Christians allow busyness to rule the day. Which, if you ask me, is the unrivalled arch-enemy of spiritual authenticity. Busyness is akin to something the Bible calls worldliness – getting caught up with society's agenda, objectives and activities to the neglect of walking with God. And whichever way you slice it, a key ingredient in authentic Christianity is time. Not leftover time, not throwaway time, but quality time. Time for contemplation, meditation and reflection. Unhurried, uninterrupted time.

## A commitment to slow down

An authentic marriage requires the same kind of time.

Many marriages are superficial. The husband becomes consumed with his job, hoping to shore up his sagging self-esteem by being impressive at work. The wife is wrapped up in the children, and she may have a job as well. And so they pass each other in the driveway, the hallway and the bathroom. They sleep in the same bed and occasionally sit at the same table, but there's not much intimacy between them. They are cohabiting, but they are not nurturing one another. They are not involved in a vital, refreshing, authentic relationship.

A few courageous couples, however, insist on more. Realizing it won't be easy, they nevertheless decide to fight for an authentic marriage. They know it will take time: they may have to give up activities that have been important to them. They know it may require some practical vehicle to help them make the change: they may need to set a recurring date night, take evening walks, toss out the TV or agree to sit at the table and talk to each other for twenty solid minutes following dinner.

Believers in Christ sometimes come to the same point in their relationships with God. 'Choked by life's worries, riches and pleasures' (Luke 8:14), they realize they are no longer growing and maturing. Their walk with Jesus has slowed to a crawl or stopped altogether.

If this has happened to you, one day you may have to say, 'That's it! I refuse merely to go through the motions of being a Christian any more. I am not going to put my Christian life on autopilot, fly through meaningless prayers and page through a Bible that I don't let saturate my life. I'm not going to play halfway games any more. I'm going to pay whatever price an authentic walk with Jesus Christ demands.'

Christians who make that commitment know that time is required. Something good is going to have to give way. Some practical vehicle will have to be employed to get the RPMs down from ten thousand to five thousand to five hundred, where they can be at peace with God and in a condition to hear what he is saying.

Friend, nobody ever said the Christian walk is easy. But is anything in this world of greater or more lasting importance?

## RPM reduction

I want to offer you a practical, tested, guaranteed RPM-reduction approach that will help you slow down your life so that you can stop playing games and begin leading an authentic Christian life.

To start, I'm going to describe a vehicle that may seem out of place in a book about prayer, but in reality is a very important first step. If your life is rushing in many directions at once, you are incapable of the kind of deep, unhurried prayer that is vital to the Christian walk. By using this vehicle, you can begin to learn to be still and know that God is God, as Psalm 46:10 exhorts.

This vehicle is keeping a journal – in this case, a spiritual journal. It involves writing down your experiences, observations and reflections; looking behind the events of the day for their hidden meanings; and recording ideas as they come to you.

When I first learned about keeping a journal, I had visions of people spending hours and hours in the middle of the day letting their stream of consciousness flow all over endless reams of paper. I wondered who on earth had this kind of discretionary time, but fortunately I kept my thoughts to myself.

Over the years I found myself drawn to the writings of a wide variety of people – mystics, Puritans, contemporary authors rich in their devotional handling of Scripture – who seemed to have one thing in common: most of them kept a journal.

In addition I began to discover something about certain people in my church and around the country whose ministries and character I deeply respect. Most of them keep a journal too. And yet I knew these people did not climb into ivory towers for the better part of the day.

## Practical journal writing

It was around this time that I read Gordon MacDonald's book *Ordering Your Private World*. In it MacDonald suggested keeping a journal, but with a twist.

Buy a spiral notebook, he said. Plan to write in this notebook every day, but restrict yourself to one page. Every day, when you open to the next blank sheet of paper, write the same first word: 'Yesterday'. Follow this with a paragraph or two recounting yesterday's events, a kind of post-match analysis.

Write whatever you want – perhaps a little description of the people you interacted with, your appointments, decisions, thoughts, feelings, high points, low points, frustrations, what you read in your Bible, what you were going to do and didn't. According to MacDonald, this exercise causes a tremendous step forward in spiritual development.

On the one hand, his approach didn't turn me completely off, as my visions of midday mystics had done. But on the other hand, I was still sceptical. 'Come on,' I thought, 'what could that exercise possibly do?'

Most of us, the author said, live unexamined lives. We repeat the same errors day after day. We don't learn much from the decisions we make, whether they are good or bad. We don't know why we're here or where we're going. One benefit of keeping a journal is to force us to examine our lives.

But an even greater benefit, he said, is this: the very act of keeping a journal – sitting down, reaching for the spiral notebook, focusing our thoughts on our life, writing for five or ten minutes – will reduce our RPMs from ten thousand to five thousand.

I knew it was just what I needed.

I have a high energy level in the morning. As I've already noted, I can't wait to get to the office to start the day's work, and once the adrenalin starts flowing, the phone starts ringing and people start arriving, I can easily stay at ten thousand RPMs until I crash at night. So I decided to start keeping a journal. What did I have to lose?

My first journal entry began, 'Yesterday I said I hated the concept of journals and I had strong suspicions about anyone who has the time to journal. I still do, but if this is what it's going to take to slow me down so I can learn to talk and walk with Christ the way I should, then I guess I'll journal.'

And I do. Every day! I don't think I've ever written anything profound in my journal, but then that's not the point. The amazing thing is what happens to my RPMs when I write. By the time I've finished a long paragraph recapping yesterday, my mind is off my responsibilities, I'm tuned in to what I'm doing and thinking, and my motor has slowed halfway down.

## A page of prayer

Keeping a journal, then, is the important first step in slowing down to pray. It gives the body a brief rest. It focuses the mind. It frees the spirit to operate, if only for a few minutes. But even though keeping a journal may improve your life enormously, it will not in and of itself turn you into an authentic Christian. It's only a first step in the right direction.

After you have bought a spiral notebook, filled the first page and reduced your RPMs by half, what's the next step? Your engine is still racing at speeds that would prove disastrous in an ordinary car.

Step two in the RPM-reduction programme is one you already know about and perhaps have even started practising. I described it in chapter 4: Write out your prayers.

Some people tell me they don't need to schedule regular time for prayer because they get by just fine by praying on the run. These people are kidding themselves. Just try building a marriage on the run. You can't build a relationship that way, with God or with another person. To get to know someone, you have to slow down and spend time together.

So, after writing in my journal has reduced my RPMs from ten thousand to five thousand, I flip all the way to the back of my spiral notebook and write a prayer. As with the journal, I limit my writing to one page. This keeps the exercise from overwhelming me and ensures that I do it every day. It also takes a realistic amount of time, given the other responsibilities I face daily.

Once I write out the prayer, I put the notebook on a low table and kneel down. Not everyone is like me in this respect, but I find I pray much more effectively on my knees. I read the prayer aloud, adding other comments or concerns as I go through it.

## Quiet enough to listen

By this time my RPMs are down to five hundred and I'm feeling really mellow. My heart is soft and I invite the Lord to speak to me by his Spirit. I'm quiet enough to hear if he chooses to speak, even if in a 'gentle whisper', as 1 Kings 19:12 says.

It's the third step to fully reducing your RPMs, this idea of listening to God. These moments in God's presence are the ones that really matter, because it is from here that authentic Christianity emanates, the unhurried, silent communing of God's Spirit with ours.

You can't become an authentic Christian on a diet of constant activity, even if the activity is all church related. Ministry, Christian rock concerts, weekend conferences, church committee meetings – these may all be valuable, but they won't serve you well as your primary source of strength. Strength is born of solitude. And in my experience decisions that change the course of your life usually come out of these holy-of-holies encounters.

To repeat what I said at the beginning of this chapter, the arch-enemy of spiritual authenticity is busyness. And if I'm correct on this, then it's time to slow down, reflect and listen.

## 12. THE IMPORTANCE OF LISTENING

I watched some motor racing a few weekends ago and was reminded that not so long ago the racing drivers were completely on their own on the track. They had to count their own laps. They had to keep straight what position they were in, figure out how much fuel they had burned and know whether they could finish the race without adding another pit stop to the equation. Because they couldn't communicate with their crew, they were left to go it alone.

But then in-helmet headsets were introduced so that drivers could communicate with their crew chiefs. How many drivers do you think took advantage of the opportunity to be in consistent communication with their crew chief? Of course all of them did.

The crew chief was on their team. The crew chief had their best interests in mind. And the crew chief had more data and a better vantage point, which dramatically increased the odds of their running a better race.

Friend, the God who wants to speak to you is on your side! He has better information than you have. He has a better vantage point than the one from where you're sitting. And he really wants you to be better in the only really important race you're ever going to be entered in: this life.

But just imagine if, right in the middle of a race, a driver called up the crew chief and went on and on about how tough the race was or how hot his suit was or how much he'd kill for an ice-cold Coke, never once allowing the chief to speak about the situation. We'd think he'd lost his mind!

'Don't you want to know what your crew chief has to say?' we'd ask. 'Don't you want to benefit from his wisdom and perspective?'

It is indeed an honour to be able to speak to God. After all, we don't have to go through a priest or a saint or any other intermediary. We don't have to follow any prescribed rituals. We don't have to wait for an appointment. Anywhere, at any time, under any circumstances, remember, we can approach his throne of grace with confidence.

But despite what most believers think, prayer is more than merely 'speaking to God'.

As I've studied prayer over the years, I've sensed God saying, 'If we are supposedly enjoying a relationship, then why are you doing all the talking? Let me get a word in somewhere!'

## God wants to speak

So, if God is so anxious to speak, how will he get it done? How does the King of the universe communicate with earthbound men and women once they allow him to get a word in edgeways?

I can think of at least three ways in which God speaks to followers who are willing to listen.

First, God speaks through his Word. As we read the Bible and meditate on its truth, God helps to apply it to our lives. A familiar verse jumps off the page at us just when we need it and seems to take on new meaning to fit our circumstances. Obviously the verse has not changed; it has always been part of God's Word. But the Holy Spirit gives it to us when it will help us the most.

Another way in which God speaks to us is through people. 'I provide for you,' he says as a neighbour shows up with a casserole we had no time to cook or money to buy. 'I care for you,' he says through the arms of a friend who understands our grief and seeks to console us. 'I guide you,' he says through a counsellor who points us to the path God has chosen for us.

And a third way in which God speaks to us is through direct promptings of the Holy Spirit. This Third Person of the Godhead is ready, willing and able to communicate with us. According to Scripture, he leads, rebukes, affirms, comforts and assures Christ's followers. But a lot of Christians don't expect God to speak to them and therefore don't believe that he does. By their actions, you'd guess Jesus had packed up and gone back to heaven forty days after his resurrection, never to be heard from again.

Though this attitude is common, it hardly fits the picture of God painted throughout Scripture.

## God spoke to Old Testament followers

Scripture is full of accounts of God speaking to his children, directly and personally. Genesis 3:8 says that God walked in the Garden of Eden 'in the cool of the day' and stopped to talk with Adam and Eve. He spoke frequently to Abraham, calling him from one place, leading him to another and promising to make of him a great nation. He talked to Moses through the burning bush, on top of Sinai and whenever Moses needed counsel in leading the children of Israel to the Promised Land. He gave Joshua military advice to enable the Israelites to conquer the fierce Canaanites. He talked with David about governing Israel and about his personal sins and struggles.

In fact, all through the Old Testament, God spoke and his people listened to – or chose to ignore – his words. The pattern is repeated in the New Testament.

## God spoke to the early church

God spoke to Saul the persecutor through a blinding light on the Damascus road. He then guided Paul the apostle as he travelled across the Roman Empire preaching the gospel. He spoke to the apostle Peter through a vision, telling him to extend Christian fellowship to a Gentile household. He spoke to the apostle John during his exile on a lonely island, showing him God's purposes in human history. Through the Holy Spirit, he guided all the members of the early church as they selected leaders, provided for each other's needs and carried the good news of Jesus Christ wherever they went.

And Jesus promised that the Holy Spirit would stay with the church for ever. Take a look at this astounding promise from John 14:16–18: 'I will ask the Father, and he will give you another Counsellor to be with you for ever – the Spirit of truth . . . I will not leave you as orphans; I will come to you.'

It makes no sense to believe that God lost his voice at the end of the first century. If the essence of Christianity is a personal relationship between the almighty God and individual human beings, it stands to reason that God still speaks to believers today. You can't build a relationship on one-way speeches. You need frequent, sustained, intimate contact between two persons, both of whom speak and both of whom listen.

Certainly, it sounds supernatural (and it is), but what's so surprising about that? The normal Christian life is defined by its supernatural dimension. As the apostle Paul says in 2 Corinthians 5:7, 'We live by faith, not by sight.'

Listening to God speak to us through his Holy Spirit is not only normal; it is essential. In Romans 8:9, Paul wrote, 'You . . . are controlled . . . by the Spirit, if the Spirit of God lives in you. And if anyone does not have the Spirit of Christ, he does not belong to Christ.'

In Galatians 5, he told believers to 'live by the Spirit', to be 'led by the Spirit' and to 'keep in step with the Spirit'.

Once a person turns his or her life over to Jesus Christ, it is no longer business as usual. Life no longer consists only of that which can be seen or smelled or felt or figured out by human logic. It includes walking by faith, and that means opening oneself to the miraculous ministry of the Holy Spirit.

## Two misguided approaches

Being open to the Spirit's activity does not involve receiving an intellectual lobotomy. You still have to choose your socks in the morning and cook your meals at night. The Spirit's promptings probably won't cover you there. In other words, Christ-followers would do well to keep straight the difference between divine promptings and earthly responsibilities.

I once met a pastor who was shocked to learn how much time I spend preparing each message I give. Ordinarily I put in from ten to twenty hours reading, studying, praying and writing out three drafts of each sermon. This pastor exclaimed, 'You go to all that trouble? I just walk into my pulpit and expect a miracle.' I was tempted to ask him if his congregation saw his sermons as miracles, but I didn't.

Don't get me wrong. As I explained in chapter 7, 'Mountain-moving prayer', I've seen God work life-changing miracles in the pulpit – even my pulpit! But be careful about putting your hands in your pockets and your brains in a drawer. Don't jump off the pinnacle and expect God to catch you just because you're already halfway down.

This form of irresponsibility is one misguided approach, but it's not the only one. Just as destructive is what I call anti-supernaturalism. The dynamic is espoused by people who are so accustomed to walking by sight, steering their own ships and making decisions apart from God that they are squeamish about letting the Holy Spirit begin his supernatural ministry in their lives. They wish for a package that was tied up a little more neatly. They would like the Spirit's ministry to be quantified and described. The Holy Spirit seems elusive and mysterious, and the whole thing unnerves them.

So, when they sense a prompting that might be from the Holy Spirit, they resist it. They analyse it and conclude, 'It isn't logical; therefore I won't pay attention to it.' In short, they question the Spirit's every prompting, guiding, rebuke and spur.

Still others want to obey the Holy Spirit, but they're just not sure how they'd know when he was really speaking. Are they hearing their own desires or God's still, small voice? Not wanting to go off the deep end, they avoid the water altogether.

All these reactions are understandable. In fact, I've often had them myself. But the results of automatically resisting supernatural promptings are usually unfortunate. People who cut themselves off from God's direction find their religious experience becoming cerebral, predictable, boring and – often – past tense.

In a later chapter we'll look at ways to tell if a prompting is truly from the Holy Spirit, which may be important for Holy Spirit enthusiasts who seem to their rationally minded friends to lack common sense. For starters, though, let's spend a few pages exploring four reasons why these promptings are so vital to the Christ-follower.

## The Spirit and eternal destiny

First, your eternal destiny is determined by how you respond to promptings from God.

If you asked several seasoned believers how they came to personal faith in Christ, you would probably find a similar pattern in their experiences. Most would refer to the mark some Christian made on their lives. Most would tell of hearing the message of Jesus Christ. And then, in almost every case, they would mention an internal nudge that drove them into the arms of Christ.

'When I heard what Jesus Christ did for me,' they might say, 'I had a feeling, an inner tug to learn more, to walk down that path to see what was at the end of it. It was as if I was being led towards Christ.'

In John 6:44, Jesus said, 'No-one can come to me unless the Father who sent me draws him.' Who draws us to Christ? God, in the person of the Holy Spirit, draws and loves and tugs and urges and leads seekers to the cross.

If you're a Christian, you can probably remember that tug from God that led you first to the cross, where you acknowledged that Christ paid for your sin, and then to repentance, forgiveness and newness of life. The wonderful thing is, even after you're a Christian, God keeps tugging!

## The Spirit and assurance

Second, promptings from the Holy Spirit are important because your assurance as a Christian depends in part on how you receive and respond to them.

When you're in an airport sometime, observe the difference between passengers who have confirmed seats and those who are on standby. The ones assured a spot read newspapers, chat with their friends or sleep. The ones on standby hang around the ticket counter and pace back and forth. The difference is caused by the confidence factor.

If you knew that in fifteen minutes you would have to stand in judgment before the Holy God and learn your eternal destiny, what would your reaction be? Would you pace nervously? Would you say to yourself, 'I don't know what God's going to say – will it be "Welcome home, child", or will it be "Depart from me; I never knew you"?'

Or would you drop to your knees and worship Jesus Christ? Would you say to yourself, 'I just can't wait, because I know God is going to open the door and invite me in'? Again, the difference is caused by the confidence factor.

What does this have to do with promptings? Paul says in Romans 8:16, 'The Spirit himself testifies with our spirit that we are God's children.' In other words, the Holy Spirit whispers and tugs and nudges and makes impressions on the spirits of true believers, and this is what he says: 'Rejoice! You've trusted Christ and now you're a member of the family. Relax! The agonizing is over; you're on the flight to heaven.'

In a hundred different ways, using all kinds of promptings, the Holy Spirit comforts and communicates with believers, convincing them that they can have absolute confidence that they are accepted into God's family.

That's the way to live – unafraid of death, because the Holy Spirit has assured you of where you will be beyond the grave. God promises that kind of assurance to his family members. If your experience is not like that, if you identify with the airport pacers, you probably haven't yet put your trust entirely in Christ. You may still be trying to earn your ticket to heaven. But your anxiety can be your best friend, if it drives you into Christ's arms for assurance of God's love for you.

## The Spirit and Christian growth

The third reason why promptings are important is this: your growth as a Christian depends on receiving and responding to promptings.

Jesus promised in John 16:13, 'When he, the Spirit of truth, comes, he will guide you into all truth.' The Holy Spirit will prompt you, tug at you and guide you as you read and heed the Word of God.

As believers, of course, we are responsible for obeying God's entire Word. But the Bible is a big book and we can't swallow it all at once. So God often gives us his truth one bite-sized piece at a time. This is certainly what he did for me.

When I became a Christian at seventeen, I sensed the Holy Spirit saying to me, 'You need to understand doctrine – the difference between grace and good works as a means of getting to heaven, the meaning of faith, the identity of God, the person of Jesus Christ and the work of the Holy Spirit.' So I studied and prayed and talked to friends and took courses on doctrinal issues.

A few years later the focus changed. Now the emphasis was on character. Every time I turned around, the Holy Spirit seemed to be saying to me, 'You need to grow in sensitivity and compassion.' I've always had a hard time being kind, gentle and tender-hearted; my personality is not naturally wired that way. And so I read and studied and memorized verses like Ephesians 4:32, which says, 'Be kind and compassionate to one another, forgiving each other, just as in Christ God forgave you.'

Later, after I married, the Holy Spirit pierced my soul as if with daggers and said, 'You are not living like a godly husband; you do not treasure your wife "as Christ loved the church and gave himself up for her" (Ephesians 5:25). Right now, the most important thing for you to learn is how to be a loving husband.'

Then it was prayer – studying how God communicates with us and what we're to do in response. Then it was another area. And next month, next year, in ten years, I'm sure he will lead me to focus on different truths altogether.

My point is, if you remain sensitive to the Holy Spirit's promptings and cooperate with them as you receive them, you can trust him to guide you into the truth and to help you grow up as a Christian. That doesn't give you licence to ignore parts of Scripture and say, 'Well, that's not what the Holy Spirit is emphasizing in my life right now.' We're responsible for hearing the whole Word of God. But you can rest assured that the Holy Spirit will emphasize just the area you need at that time.

## The Spirit and guidance

The fourth reason why you need to be attuned to the promptings of the Holy Spirit is that your life plans are greatly affected by how you receive and respond to God's promptings.

You matter to God. He made you and he knows what will fulfil you. He knows what vocation is best suited to your talents and abilities. He knows whether you should marry or remain single, and if you marry, he knows which marriage partner is best suited to you. He knows what church you can flourish in. And this is what he says to you: 'I want to guide your life. I know the path that will glorify me and be productive for you, and I want to put you on it. I'll do that primarily through promptings, so quieten your life, please. Just listen to me.'

# 13. HOW TO HEAR GOD'S PROMPTINGS

The Spirit nudges us to accept God's offer of salvation, assures us that we are members of God's eternal family, encourages us to grow and guides us along the path God has chosen for us. Suffice it to say, hearing the Holy Spirit's promptings is vitally important to leading a healthy Christian life.

But often, when the Spirit tries to get through to us, he gets a busy signal in return. For many of us, something's got to change!

## The discipline of stillness

People who are truly interested in hearing from God understand that there is a price to be paid, which usually comes in the form of disciplined stillness. (If you're cringing at the mere mention of being still, this chapter is for you!)

If anyone could have played the I-don't-have-time-to-be-still card, it was Jesus. Crowds followed him wherever he went, and his preaching/teaching/healing ministry was an all-day, everyday occurrence. Yet Jesus developed the discipline of stillness before God in spite of the roles and responsibilities he carried.

Mark 1:35 tells us, 'Very early in the morning, while it was still dark, Jesus got up, left the house and went off to a solitary place, where he prayed.' So, obviously, times of stillness and solitude were important to him. In those times of seclusion he not only poured out his heart to the Father, but he earnestly listened to him as well. He needed his Father's comfort, direction, affirmation and assurance. And because of the continual promptings he received from the Father, there was purpose to his steps. The people around him saw his confidence and certainty, and they were amazed 'because he taught them as one who had authority' (Mark 1:22).

If Jesus were the only person mentioned in Scripture who took time to listen to the Lord, the example would be strong enough for us to follow. But that isn't the case at all. King David, author of many of the psalms, 'went in and sat before the Lord'. The prophet Isaiah, before taking on an immensely difficult commission from God, listened to God in his temple (Isaiah 6). The apostle Peter 'went up on the roof to pray' at lunchtime, and God talked to him there (Acts 10:9–20).

Scripture is full of accounts of people who took time to hear what God had to say to them.

## Strength from solitude

God's power is available to us when we come to him in solitude, when we learn how to focus and centre our hearts and be quiet before him. When we learn the discipline of stillness before God, we find that his promptings come through to us clearly and with little interference.

After a long season of trying to pray and receive God's

promptings on the run, it became obvious to me that the pace of my life had outstripped my capacity to analyse it. It exhausted me to be constantly doing and rarely reflecting on what I had done. At the end of a day, I'd wonder if my work had any meaning at all.

I finally grew so tired of leading an unexamined life that I made a commitment to spend from half an hour to an hour every morning in a secluded place with the Lord. There are no merit badges associated with the practice, but my life became vastly richer as a result of it.

After I reflect on the previous day and write out my prayers, my spirit is quiet and receptive. That is when I write an L for listen on a piece of paper and circle it. Then I sit quietly and simply say, 'Now, Lord, I invite you to speak to me by your Holy Spirit.'

This manner of quietening my mind and preparing myself to hear God speak works well for me, but I know it won't work for everyone. Some people can't stand writing anything, let alone journals and prayers. They may prefer to talk quietly to God. Some are good at meditating without writing or saying a word.

The important thing is not to force a particular method, but instead to find a way that works for you. Custom-fit an approach that will still your racing mind and frenetic body, soften your heart and enable you to hear God's still, small voice. Then, when you are centred and focused on God, invite him to speak to you.

## Questions for God

After years and years of engaging in these meaningful conversations with God, I've noticed that several questions tend to crop up when I'm inviting him to speak. The first is, 'What's the next step in developing my character?' I almost always hear from God when I ask that question, because there's always an edge of my life he is trying to round out.

Another is, 'What's the next step in my family – with Lynne and the children?' I generally receive a lot of direction from God in this area too. Throughout my entire ministry, my wife has been supportive of me, and it's as if God says, 'You'd better return that. Try to serve her as enthusiastically as she serves you.'

A third question is, 'What's the next step in my ministry?' I have no idea how people in ministry survive without listening to God. Most of my creative ideas for messages and programmes and new directions come from my morning time with him.

Depending on your situation, you might ask, 'What's the next step in my vocation?' Or 'In what direction should my dating relationship go?' Or 'What should I do for my children?' Or 'How should I further my education?' Or 'How should I plan my giving?'

Whatever you ask the Lord, you will be amazed by the way he leads. Once you are quiet and tender before him, waiting to hear him speak, he will bring a verse to mind or will guide you through your thoughts and feelings. As you build the discipline of stillness into your life, you will find these quiet moments in God's presence becoming incredibly precious to you.

## Answers from God

Suppose that right after reading this chapter you put down the book and quieten your spirit before God. You wait until you are focused on him and then you say, as the young prophet Samuel said, 'Speak, LORD, for your servant is listening' (1 Samuel 3:9). In the solitude and stillness, what might God say to you?

To some seekers, God might say, 'You've been reading Christian books and going to Christian meetings long enough. Now it's time you became a Christian. Come to me, repent of your sin and enter into a faith-orientated relationship with me.'

To those who have already made that commitment, he might say, 'Return to me. You've been stumbling and bumbling around. It's been a long, dry summer. Let's get reacquainted. Let's have fellowship again!'

To people facing trials, he might offer words of comfort: 'I'm right here. I know your name and I know your pain. I'm going to give you strength . . . please trust me.'

To others, faithful through hardships, he might say, 'I am so pleased with you! I'm glad you are being faithful even though life is difficult for you. Keep it up!'

And to still others, this message might come: 'Follow my promptings and take a risk. Try this new direction. Face this new challenge. Walk with me towards new horizons.'

The message will be suited to the person's individual need, but the central truth is certain: we serve a God who has spoken in history, who will indeed speak tomorrow and who wants to speak to us right now, right where we are.

## When God is silent

But what if no message comes through?

Sometimes, when I wait quietly for God to speak, I sense total silence from heaven. It's as if no-one's home, which makes me feel more than a little silly. My thoughts get the better of me: 'Did I ask the wrong question? Was I foolish to expect answers? Was God really listening?'

After thinking about this issue for a long time, though, I've concluded that I don't need to feel upset if sometimes God chooses to remain silent. He's a living Being, not an answering machine. He speaks when he has something to say.

On several occasions during the course of a typical month, I'll ask my wife, 'Is there anything you want to tell me that we haven't had time to sit down and talk about?' My question gives Lynne an opportunity to tell me anything she wants, but it doesn't force her to talk. Sometimes she says, 'No, nothing in particular.' And that's fine. More often than not, though, she does have a message for me – and so does God, when I consistently invite him to speak.

## Tuned in to God's voice

I know that God continues to speak to his people today, and I am convinced that there are two reasons why we don't hear his voice more often. The most obvious reason is that we don't listen for it. We don't schedule times of stillness that make communication possible.

Be honest with yourself. When do you turn off the TV, the radio and your iPod and listen to nothing louder than the refrigerator's hum? When do you turn off the sound track of your mind and come away from the numbers, machines, words, schemes or whatever it is that occupies your waking thoughts? When do you make yourself quiet and available to God? When do you formally invite him to speak to you?

Do you build the discipline of solitude into your schedule? Try it! Like any new practice, it will feel awkward at first. But gradually it will become more natural, and eventually you'll feel off balance if you don't make time for solitude every day.

In addition to carving out blocks of time to listen to God, do you keep your ears tuned to him each day? A friend of mine has a company car equipped with a radio, a CD player, a phone and a mobile communication unit that he monitors at a very low decibel level when he's in the car. Often we've been riding along together, talking and listening to music, when all of a sudden he'll reach down, pick up the microphone and say, 'I'm here; what's up?'

With all the other noise in the car, I never hear the mobile unit's signal. But he has tuned his ear to it. He is able to carry on a conversation and listen to music without ever losing his awareness that a call may come over that unit.

It is possible to develop a similar sensitivity to the Holy Spirit's still, small voice. It is possible to be aware of God's gentle promptings throughout the day, even while going about your daily work.

## Moment by moment

These on-the-spot promptings, however, are not a substitute for unhurried quiet time with God. In fact, they tend to come to me only when I regularly make time for stillness and solitude.

Say you're driving to a sales call, and as if out of nowhere you sense God by his Holy Spirit saying, 'Aren't you glad you're my child? Aren't you glad you have a home in heaven? Aren't you glad I'm with you right now? Don't you feel safe and secure in my presence?' When you process a communication like that, the whole world seems to evaporate; your car becomes a sanctuary, and it's just you and the Lord enjoying each other. How people live without moments like that, I don't know.

## Listen and obey

The other reason why we may not hear God's voice is that we don't plan to do anything about it. God speaks, we listen and nod and we say, 'How interesting!' But if we don't follow up on the Holy Spirit's promptings, he may see no reason to continue speaking. The next chapter is all about discerning God's voice and choosing to obey.

People who make opportunities for the Holy Spirit to speak to them know that the Christian life is a continual adventure. It is full of surprises, thrills, challenges and mysteries. If you open your mind and heart to God's promptings, you will be amazed at what he will do. He is attempting to communicate with you more often than you know. You have no idea how much richer and fuller, how much more exciting and more effective your life will be once you make the decision to be still, to be aware and to obey God's promptings.

# GOD PROMPTS US TO ACTION

# 14. WHAT TO DO WITH PROMPTINGS

After a particularly exhausting meeting one evening, I got into my car to head home. As I made my way down the exit road, I noticed out of the corner of my eye someone walking towards the parking area. In that fraction of a second I received what I thought was a prompting from God – to go and offer some form of assistance to the person I had just passed.

My initial response was 'Why?' The person didn't seem to be having any difficulty. My second response was 'Why me?' I'd already done my share that day, studying, working on a sermon, counselling people and then leading a meeting. I just wanted to go home.

And so I kept driving, rationalizing my disobedience to the little prompting from God with every quarter of a mile gained. But wouldn't you know, the Holy Spirit persisted. By the time I had reached the entrance sign to Willow's property, I felt so restless in my spirit that I decided I couldn't put up with it any more. Disobedience was causing more stress than simply turning round and obeying, even if I was tired and even if I did deserve to go home.

I headed back down the entrance road, pulled alongside the person, who was still walking, rolled my window down and said awkwardly, 'Is there any way I can serve you? Could I drive you to your car or something?'

I'd never seen the woman before, but she recognized me and gladly accepted my offer. We drove towards her car, and just as she was about to thank me and step out, she said, 'There was an announcement in the bulletin at church tonight about the need for administrative help in the church office, and I've been feeling God leading me to apply for that position. What do you think?'

That night I had no idea how offering help to a person who probably didn't need it would affect my life and ministry. As it turned out, the woman joined our staff and served faithfully for almost ten years.

I cringe when I imagine what Willow might have missed if I hadn't obeyed that prompting.

## Private promptings

I was once attending a conference in southern California where, for some strange reason, I felt I ought to attend a workshop in which I had very little interest. The workshop was in a different building, and as I was walking to it, I met a young man and started talking with him.

As we talked, I was impressed by his tender spirit, and I realized God was knitting our hearts together. Over the course of several months, we corresponded and then agreed to meet again in person. Eventually he joined our church staff and built one of the most effective youth ministries in the country.

Friend, when God tells you to write to this person, or make

an appointment with that person, or give away so much money, to start this, or stop that, or share the other thing, it doesn't have to make sense. Some of the most important decisions in my life have made no sense at all from a worldly perspective. But I have learned that I can't afford not to respond to the Spirit's promptings.

One morning an elder of my church called me on the phone and said, 'I had a prompting to call you. Are you in trouble or anything?'

I thought about her question for a split second. 'Not that I know of.'

'All right,' she said. 'I'm just obeying the Lord. I wanted to call you and encourage you.'

I was glad she called, even if neither of us knew exactly why. I never object to being encouraged, and I was glad she was obedient to the Holy Spirit.

When God tells us to do something, as long as it's within the limits set by Scripture, we don't have to understand it. All we need to do is obey . . . and then trust God to use our obedience to accomplish his will.

Promptings are intensely private phenomena. You get them and I get them, but unless we share them, nobody knows what we do with them. I could have disobeyed that prompting to help the woman in the car park and nobody would have known. I could have ignored the feeling that I ought to attend the workshop that didn't interest me and nobody would have written a news story about it.

In fact, if I had paid no attention to those promptings, I would never have known what I missed. How could I know that the person in the car park was just the capable administrative assistant our staff needed, or that on my way to the workshop I would run into the best possible youth minister for my church?

I could tell story after story of promptings God has entrusted to me and to others. I could describe the dramatic effects of obeying God's promptings – or of ignoring them. But such stories may not be to the point. The real question is this: What are you going to do about the promptings you receive?

## Is it really from God?

When I raise this question, people sometimes ask me a question in return. 'I believe in promptings,' they say. 'I am willing to obey. In fact, I have often done so. But I know that there are other spirits loose in this world and they aren't all holy. I also know that I am capable of thinking that my own intense desires are the Holy Spirit's wishes. How can I be sure that a prompting is truly from God?'

It's a valid question because the Bible warns us that Satan, the evil one, is capable of both issuing his own promptings for destructive purposes and undermining God's promptings in your life. Paul wrote in 1 Timothy 4:1, 'The Spirit clearly says that in later times some will abandon the faith and follow deceiving spirits and things taught by demons.'

These lying spirits may appear to be channels of God's power. John referred to 'spirits of demons performing miraculous signs' (Revelation 16:14). And Jesus predicted that 'false Christs and false prophets' would 'perform great signs and miracles to deceive even the elect – if that were possible' (Matthew 24:24).

Evil spirits are not necessarily easy to distinguish from God's ministering spirits, the angels. As Paul pointed out, 'Satan himself masquerades as an angel of light' (2 Corinthians 11:14). So of course it is very important to know the origin of the promptings coming into your mind.

In the third chapter of Genesis, Adam and Eve followed a

prompting to increase their knowledge by eating an attractive fruit, and they plunged the human race into darkness and misery. King David followed a prompting to befriend a beautiful army wife, and it cost him his best general and a son (2 Samuel 11 – 12).

Who led Lee Harvey Oswald to shoot President Kennedy, led Idi Amin to exterminate many of his fellow citizens in Uganda, led a bunch of radical martyrs to blow up the World Trade Center, or led a platoon of American GIs to massacre the women and children of My Lai? Who leads the Ku Klux Klan to throw rocks and bottles at their neighbours because their skin is darker than their own? Who leads me to say hurtful things, to be arrogant, to colour the truth? Who prompts me to care less about service to others than about my own advancement and fulfilment?

## Heavenly warfare

In Ephesians 6:10–18, Paul reminds us that there's a war going on in this universe.

> Put on the full armour of God, so that you can take your stand against the devil's schemes. For our struggle is not against flesh and blood, but against the rulers, against the authorities, against the powers of this dark world and against the spiritual forces of evil in the heavenly realms. (Ephesians 6:11–12)

This war is being waged on the spiritual battlefields of our minds. As God leads people for his glory and for their benefit, Satan does everything in his power to undo God's work and undermine his activity in people's lives. Because of this spiritual war, it is possible that some of the notions that come into our heads have been authored in hell, not heaven.

There are only two ways to respond to devilish promptings: flight or fight. 'Flee the evil desires of youth,' Paul told the youthful Timothy in 2 Timothy 2:22. 'Resist the devil, and he will flee from you,' James wrote in James 4:7.

But how can you be sure where a particular prompting is coming from? In 1 John 4:1, we read, 'Dear friends, do not believe every spirit, but test the spirits to see whether they are from God, because many false prophets have gone out into the world.'

The following are three criteria that have served me well when testing the promptings I receive.

## Consistent with Scripture

First, all promptings that come from God are consistent with his Word, the Bible.

The surest way to test the source of a prompting is to check it against Scripture. As I interact with people in my church, almost every month someone tells me of his or her unfaithfulness to a spouse and how God 'is OK with it'.

They think they are being led to their perfect mates (by way of an affair, mind you), hand-picked by God himself, and that their present marriages are nothing more than regrettable mistakes. The only way they can do God's will, they tell me, is to repent of the sin (read: 'my current marriage') and be united with 'the one I should have married in the first place'.

The rationalizations are often sophisticated, but the bottom line is always the same – people want to divorce the spouses to whom they were joined in holy matrimony in order to marry others who seem more attractive. This is not a prompting from God. I can say that unequivocally because of what God has to say on the matter: 'May you rejoice in the wife of your youth . . . May you ever be captivated by her love. Why be captivated, my son, by an adulteress?' (Proverbs 5:18–20)

Or what about this one from Malachi 2:13–14, 16?

> [The Lord] no longer pays attention to your offerings or accepts them with pleasure from your hands. You ask, 'Why?' It is because the LORD is acting as the witness between you and the wife of your youth, because you have broken faith with her, though she is your partner, the wife of your marriage covenant . . . 'I hate divorce,' says the LORD God of Israel.

A prompting to be unfaithful to your spouse is never a prompting from God. Should I say that again? A prompting to be unfaithful to your spouse is never a prompting from God. Neither is a prompting to cheat in an examination, to exaggerate to a customer, to spread hurtful gossip, to deceive your parents or your children, or to do anything else forbidden by Scripture.

If the prompting goes against the Bible, it obviously comes from an unholy spirit. Call it satanic and dismiss it summarily. There is no other way to deal with an unscriptural prompting.

## Consistent with God's gifts

On the other hand, a prompting may be consistent with God's Word and still not be sent by the Holy Spirit. For example, nothing in the Bible told Jesus he should not turn stones into bread, as the devil was urging him to do. He had other reasons for refusing to do what Satan said.

If a prompting is not contrary to Scripture, it's time to look at the second criterion: God's promptings are usually consistent with the person he made you to be.

Some people seem to think that God creates a person with

certain gifts and then expects the person to excel in totally unrelated fields. I've met people who thrive in maths and the computer field, but who assume God is prompting them to go into music or theology.

Some people who love the outdoors and don't really come alive unless they're experiencing nature nevertheless assume God is nudging them towards a nine-to-five office job in a high-rise city building.

I've even met people who are uncomfortable around children and who still think God is prompting them to become schoolteachers.

I ask these people why they assume God's promptings would contradict who he made them to be. 'Why would he design you for one purpose and then ask you to fulfil another?'

Our God is purposeful. He is the master orchestrator and synthesizer of the universe. To be sure, he loves to stretch our abilities and expand our potential, and that often involves pushing us along untried paths, but that does not mean that he ignores our gifts and inherent interests. After all, he gave them to us in the first place so that we could serve him more effectively. Instead he strengthens our natural abilities and builds on them.

If you sense a prompting that seems contrary to who God made you to be, I advise you to test it carefully. Is God asking you to do this difficult thing because there is no-one else who will do it? Is he asking you to stretch into new areas so that your unique gifts will grow? Or is this perhaps not a God-inspired prompting at all, but rather a distraction from the task God has given you to do?

## The servanthood dimension

Third, God's promptings usually involve servanthood. I find that many counterfeit promptings are fairly easy to discern, because they are self-promoting or self-serving. It never fails – in late January or early February, when the Midwest of America goes into the deep freeze, I feel a strange but compelling calling to start a church in Honolulu.

A frustrated man called me recently and said, 'I've been an elder in my church for thirty years, and I've seen a lot of pastors come and go. I'd like to know why every one of them has felt a prompting to leave this church when the invitation elsewhere involved more money, more benefits, a bigger staff and a larger house. No pastor has ever been led to a smaller church with a smaller salary and fewer benefits.'

Over the years I've found that if a prompting promises easy money and fame and perks and toys, I'd better watch out. Prosperity has ruined more people than servanthood and adversity ever will. On the other hand, I can usually sense that a prompting is from the Holy Spirit when it calls me to humble myself, serve somebody, encourage somebody or give something away. Rarely will the evil one lead us to do those kinds of things.

Paul told the Ephesian elders about one of his promptings: 'Now, compelled by the Spirit, I am going to Jerusalem, not knowing what will happen to me there. I only know that in every city the Holy Spirit warns me that prison and hardships are facing me' (Acts 20:22–23).

Paul was not being asked to do something contrary to his gifts – all the way to Jerusalem he would be preaching the gospel and strengthening young churches. He was, however, being asked to sacrifice safety and comfort for the sake of the kingdom.

Not every prompting from God will involve pain and sacrifice, but expect that quite often God's promptings will mean making gut-wrenching decisions that test the limits of your faith and make you face life's ultimate issues head-on. Many of God's promptings will require you to choose between being comfortable and building a godly character, amassing money and seeking first God's kingdom, being a winner in the world's eyes and being a winner in God's eyes.

So, if a prompting promises you overnight health, wealth, comfort and happiness, be cautious. God led Jesus to a cross, not a crown, and yet that cross ultimately proved to be the gateway to freedom and forgiveness for every sinner in the world. God also asks us, as Jesus' followers, to carry a cross. Paradoxically, in carrying that cross, we find liberty and joy and fulfilment.

## Proceed with caution

Can I add a few cautions as we close out this idea?

- If a prompting requires you to make a major, life-changing decision in a very short period of time, question it.
- If a prompting requires you to go deeply into debt or place someone else in a position of awkwardness, compromise or danger, question it.
- If a prompting requires you to jeopardize – not to mention, shatter – family relationships or important friendships, question it.
- If a prompting creates unrest in the spirits of mature Christian friends or counsellors as you share it with them, question it.

I'm not saying you should automatically reject such promptings unless they are also against Scripture, but reconsider them and treat them very carefully. Promptings from God can open the door to a fantastically fulfilling Christian adventure, but counterfeit promptings can cause unbelievable amounts of confusion, hardship, pain and trauma.

## Test and obey

I'd like to end on a positive note, so let me affirm that, while it is a terrible loss when Christians are so afraid of counterfeit promptings that they close their ears to the Holy Spirit's promptings, God does want us to test the spirits. What's more, once they are tested, he desires that we step out in faith and follow him.

Some years ago I had lunch at a restaurant with a man who was not a believer. His friends had told me that he was the toughest, hardest hitting, most autocratic, hard-headed, hard-hearted man they had ever met. (With a recommendation like that, I didn't bother to check with his enemies.) Twenty minutes into the meal, I could affirm everything they had said.

We were talking about ridiculously trivial matters when I felt a prompting. The Holy Spirit seemed to whisper to me, 'Present the simple truth of Jesus dying for sinners as clearly as you possibly can right now.'

I didn't want to do that.

I thought I knew for certain what his response would be. But the prompting was certainly biblical. It fit my gifts, at least under other circumstances, and trust me, it was not in any way self-serving.

I had a choice: would I trust God, or would I disobey this prompting that seemed to be from him?

Well, I obeyed. Abruptly changing the subject, I asked, 'Would you like to know how Jesus Christ takes sinners to heaven?'

'Pardon me?' said the man.

'Point of information,' I said. 'Would you like to know how Jesus Christ forgives sinners and takes them to heaven?'

'I guess so,' he reluctantly agreed.

So, over dessert, I explained the plan of salvation as plainly and as briefly as I knew how. He asked a few questions. We finished lunch and I went back to work feeling slightly embarrassed.

Two or three days later I almost fell off my chair when the man called me. He said, 'Do you know what I did after our lunch together? I went into my bedroom, got on my knees and said, "I'm a sinner in need of a Saviour."'

That man became a strong Christian. His spirit mellowed and he became one of my closest friends. We had seven wonderful years of fellowship together before he went to be with the Lord. And it can all be traced back to a simple, God-given prompting.

When you begin to listen for God's promptings, you often won't know why he is asking you to do something. He will lead you down paths through unknown territory, sometimes for no other reason than to teach you to trust him. But for a truly dynamic, authentic, exciting Christian life, you simply must listen for the Holy Spirit's promptings. Listen for all you're worth. And then test them. Obey them. Roll the spiritual dice and take a faith gamble, if you care to think of it that way. Say 'yes' to cooperating with God even if it seems risky or illogical.

I promise this much: you will be amazed at what he will do.

# 15. LIVING IN GOD'S PRESENCE

In college I met a professor who was always able to capture my attention. Most of the time, when discussing matters pertaining to God, it seemed as if he'd just had lunch with him. As if he and God had just stopped at Burger King en route to the campus and grabbed a quick bite. It was that conversational, that intimate.

To this professor, Jesus was a brother. A friend.

I couldn't understand that type of relationship with the 'immortal, invisible, God only wise, in light inaccessible hid from our eyes', to quote the well-known hymn – but I wanted it. And so I started hanging around the professor after class. One day I got up the courage to ask him how he seemed to know Christ in a way that I didn't.

His answer clicked in my mind: 'Maybe you understand Jesus only as the forgiver of your sins and you neglect to know him in any other way.'

The professor was right. A few years earlier I'd admitted

my sinfulness and recognized my need for a Saviour. I had bent the knee to Christ, and he had cleansed me. Grateful for his grace in my life, I had been praying, 'O Lord, thank you for dying on the cross to forgive my sins.'

But besides relating to Jesus as forgiver and as Lord of my life, I hadn't been relating to him as he asked us to in John 15:15: 'I no longer call you servants, because a servant does not know his master's business. Instead, I have called you friends, for everything that I learned from my Father I have made known to you.'

To be sure, the purpose of prayer is not simply to draw up one's requests and praises and present them in an acceptable fashion to God. It is not simply to become aware of God's answers and guidance. God doesn't instruct us to pray without ceasing just so that he can easily send us revised directions whenever needed.

The purpose of prayer goes deeper than that. Prayer is a way to maintain constant communion with God the Father and God the Son through God the Holy Spirit. It is the means of living out the intense relationship Jesus described in John 15:5–8:

> I am the vine, you are the branches. Those who abide in me and I in them bear much fruit, because apart from me you can do nothing. Whoever does not abide in me is thrown away like a branch and withers; such branches are gathered, thrown into the fire, and burned. If you abide in me, and my words abide in you, ask for whatever you wish, and it will be done for you. My Father is glorified by this, that you bear much fruit, and become my disciples. (NRSV)

A book about prayer would be incomplete without mention of God's abiding presence with his followers. Prayer and

God's presence are two sides of the same coin. Awareness of God's presence comes as the result of taking time to speak and listen to him through prayer; conversely, the power of prayer is unleashed in the lives of those who spend time in God's presence.

Too many Christians know a lot about God but rarely or never experience his presence in their lives. I was raised in a denomination that stresses God's transcendence. We thought of God in lofty and exalted terms, as well we should, but we overemphasized that side of him. He seemed lifted up far above his creatures and worshippers, and the distance between us often seemed unbridgeable.

I knew what it meant to fear God, and I understood the importance of serving him. I expected one day to stand under his judgment, believing it was my duty to obey his commandments. But one thing was sorely lacking in my Christian experience: any real understanding of the close relationship God wishes to have with his children.

## Practising the presence

'If Jesus were to explain this verse to you personally,' the professor told me, 'this is what he might say: "I want to relate to you as your forgiver and Lord, but I also want to be your friend. I want our conversations to bring you comfort. I'd like our dialogues to have some give and take. I'd like you to think about me during your day. I want you to know you're never alone, to feel that wherever you go and whatever you do, there's a companion by your side. I want you to discover my presence in your daily life."'

Brother Lawrence, a cook in a seventeenth-century French monastery, gave the world a phrase that well describes such a deep friendship with Jesus: the practice of the presence of God. As this humble monk washed dishes and served food to his brothers, he communed with God, and the glow of God's presence gave his menial kitchen duties richness and significance.

I discovered Brother Lawrence's book at about the time my professor was challenging me to get acquainted with Jesus as a friend, and from the monk's book and my professor's teachings and example, I gradually became aware of God's presence in my own life. From Brother Lawrence, I learned that in my car, on the job, at home, while working out, while helping somebody move, while lying in bed at night, at any time, anywhere, under any circumstances, I could commune meaningfully with the Lord. God was near me and wanted to enjoy a friendship with me through his Son, Jesus.

## God's presence in history

Going to the Bible, I discovered that throughout recorded history God has taken pains to let his people know of his presence among them.

After leading the Israelites out of Egypt and into the desert, God knew they would feel frightened and alone. Responsible for their children and livestock, they were camping in a place with wild animals, little food and practically no water. They had no armies and no walls to protect them from enemy attack. They didn't even know the way to the Promised Land.

In their heads they knew they were God's people and he had promised to protect them. But it was hard to feel his presence. And so God, wanting to convince them that he was with them wherever they went, gave them a visible sign of his presence. 'By day the LORD went ahead of them in a pillar of cloud to guide them on their way and by night in a pillar of fire to give them light' (Exodus 13:21).

If ever the people began to wonder if their journey was

heading in the right direction, all they had to do was look up and see the pillar of cloud. If ever they grew frightened of animals or enemies that might be stalking them by night, all they had to do was look at the pillar of fire casting its glow over the camp. God made sure they could feel his presence in their midst.

The Old Testament tells of many ways God let his people know he was among them: through the tabernacle that accompanied Israel on its journeys, through his Shekinah glory that rested over the ark in the temple, through a whole succession of prophets who spoke his word to the people. But the fullness of God's presence was yet to come.

## God with us

The New Testament begins with God offering us his presence in the person of Jesus Christ, his Son.

The promised baby was to be called Immanuel, and John explains the significance of Jesus' birth by explaining, 'The Word became flesh and made his dwelling among us' (John 1:14). Theologians call this the incarnation – God putting on human flesh and living with his people.

God's presence on earth through Jesus Christ was not some otherworldly, mystical phenomenon. It was not something that could be discerned only by priests, prophets or intellectuals. John emphasized the physical reality of the incarnation in 1 John 1:1–2:

> That which was from the beginning, which we have heard, which we have seen with our eyes, which we have looked at and our hands have touched – this we proclaim concerning the Word of life. The life appeared; we have seen it and testify to it, and we proclaim to you the eternal life, which was with the Father and has appeared to us.

God's presence through Jesus was powerful. It transformed ordinary, sinful people into apostles who 'turned the world upside down', as Acts 17:6 says (KJV). Even unbelieving leaders recognized what made the difference in these men: 'When they saw the courage of Peter and John and realized that they were unschooled, ordinary men, they were astonished and they took note that these men had been with Jesus' (Acts 4:13).

## Christ in you

But as powerful as God's presence in Christ was, it still lacked something. Jesus' ministry on earth lasted only about three years. He never left Palestine. Only a relatively small number of people ever met him personally, which means the vast majority of people who have lived on earth have never come into direct contact with him. For this reason Jesus promised his disciples, 'I will ask the Father, and he will give you another Counsellor to be with you for ever – the Spirit of truth' (John 14:16–17).

Shortly after Jesus ascended to the Father, that promise was fulfilled. On the day of Pentecost, God sent the Holy Spirit to take up permanent residence in the lives of believers. And ever since Pentecost, all believers have a strong sign of God's presence with them.

The moment you surrender to Christ and become his, God cleanses you of your sin and simultaneously fills you with his Holy Spirit. The indwelling Spirit then begins broadcasting to your own spirit a non-stop signal proclaiming God's presence in your life. Over a period of time, you grow to realize that you are never alone. God's presence is real. You can feel it because it is with you wherever you go.

When you practise being aware of God's presence, you pick up his signals all through the day. At work, at home, in your car, or wherever you are, you begin to have a dialogue with the Lord. You share your heart with him and you know he's listening. It has nothing to do with being in a church building or on your knees. It has to do with God's presence in and around you – 'Christ in you,' Colossians 1:27 says, 'the hope of glory.'

## A faithful friend

When you increase your awareness of God's presence, you gain divine companionship.

You don't have to live long to discover that God created people to thrive on companionship. Children love to play with friends, and adolescents enjoy socializing. Adults maintain relationships with friends and colleagues and make lifetime commitments to a spouse and children.

No matter how many or how deep your friendships, however, at some point you begin to realize that human companionship is not enough. Even the best of friends can't be around you all the time. They move away, fade away or die. They don't always understand what you are going through. They aren't always faithful and dependable. In short, if you try to meet all your companionship needs through human beings, you are doomed to perpetual, unfulfilled yearnings.

But God does not expect us to have only human friends. Proverbs 18:24 says, 'There is a friend who sticks closer than a brother.' Hebrews 4:15 tells us that Jesus, having been 'tempted in every way, just as we are', understands us completely. Psalm 121:3 assures us that our divine friend is always available to us: 'He who watches over you will not slumber.' Your heavenly Friend always listens. He freely communicates with you without barriers. When he expresses affection, he means it. He is patient with your immaturity, forgives you when you wrong him and stays committed to you even when you ignore him for long periods of time. He is always faithful.

## A basis for trust

A second benefit that comes from cultivating a relationship with Christ and living in his presence is supernatural confidence.

Companionship is wonderful. Even more wonderful is realizing who your closest companion is – God Almighty, the Creator and Sustainer of the universe, able to empower you to face anything that comes your way.

When I was a young teenager learning to sail my dad's boat, I'd often take a friend out on Lake Michigan. If I saw a threatening cloud formation coming our way, however, or if the winds began feeling a bit strong, I'd quickly take the sails down and head for the shore. It was nice having a pal with me. The companionship was pleasant. But in a storm my inexperienced crew would be no good to me at all.

At other times, my dad and I would sail together. Again I'd take the helm, but with Dad in the boat, I looked eagerly for cloud formations and heavy winds. My dad had sailed across the Atlantic Ocean, had survived five days of hurricane and was able to handle anything Lake Michigan could throw at us. With him on board, I had both companionship and confidence.

As you enjoy God's presence in your life, you become increasingly aware of your companion's identity and character and strength. Nothing is too difficult for God to handle. There are no limits to his power. Life can't throw anything at you that you can't handle with God.

You may be experiencing clear sailing right now. Having the all-powerful God as your companion may not seem very important. But I'll guarantee you that your life will not be free of storms – nobody's is. Between today and the day you die, you are going to have your share of heartbreak, disappointment, trial and tragedy. Know that with God's presence in your life, you will be able to face these storms with confidence.

### Love one another

A third benefit of practising the presence of God is increased compassion for other human beings.

The more time you spend with Christ, the more you begin to act like him. People matter to Jesus, and what matters to him matters to his followers. His concern and compassion begin to rub off on you.

Look at what happened to the apostle John. At one point he wanted to destroy a whole city because some of its residents didn't want Jesus to stay there (Luke 9:54). After a lifetime in God's presence, John wrote, 'Whoever does not love does not know God, because God is love' (1 John 4:8).

Or look at Peter, the apostle who, even after Pentecost, couldn't bear to associate with certain people (Galatians 2:11–14). In his famous 'ladder' of Christian virtues he shows how Christlike character develops: 'Add to your faith goodness; and to goodness, knowledge; and to knowledge, self-control; and to self-control, perseverance; and to perseverance, godliness; and to godliness, brotherly kindness; and to brotherly kindness, love' (2 Peter 1:5–7). Through his lifelong association with Christ, Peter came to value brotherly kindness and love. He knew that it is God who helps us grow in brotherly kindness and at the same time makes us aware of his presence through the compassion and love of other Christians.

I travelled many miles to speak at a conference once. Just as I was leaving my hotel room, the phone rang. It was a Christian brother from my home town, and he had tracked me down in the middle of his working day just to say, 'I want you to remember that whatever you're doing today, God is with you and so am I. I'm standing behind you and praying for you.'

Through my friend's caring I felt God's presence all through the conference. And I knew that my friend was able to minister to me because God was present in his life too.

That's one way in which Christ is building his kingdom – by instilling his compassion in the hearts of all his followers, who then minister to each other and to the whole world. In the Old Testament, God was present in his temple. Since Pentecost, we have become his temple (1 Corinthians 3:16), and our concern for others helps them understand and feel God's presence.

## Enjoy him for ever

And that brings us back to the Lord's Prayer: 'Thy kingdom come, thy will be done on earth as it is in heaven.' What is God's will, then? First and foremost, that we would believe in his love and power. But also that we come to him in sincerity and trust; that we would clear away barriers between us, including preoccupation and excessive busyness; that we'd listen for his still, small voice and obey it when we hear it; and that we would live in his presence and enjoy him for ever.

Prayer is the way to turn dry theological descriptions into warm, living, personal realities. When we live in constant communion with God, our needs are met, our faith increases and our love expands. We begin to feel God's peace in our hearts, and we spontaneously worship him.

With the heavenly beings described in Revelation, we cry out, 'Worthy is the Lamb, who was slain, to receive power and wealth and wisdom and strength and honour and glory and praise! . . . To him who sits on the throne and to the Lamb be praise and honour and glory and power, for ever and ever!' (5:12–13)

I'm enjoying God more and more these days. He answers my prayers. He empowers me. He gives me insights from his Word. He guides my life. He gives me loving relationships. And what's more, he has wonderful things in store for me on the road ahead.

My life with God is a constant adventure, and it all begins with prayer. Regular prayer, early in the morning, alone with him. Prayer that listens as well as speaks.

You, too, can enjoy God, as he created you to do. You can feel his companionship, his capability, his compassion on an ever-increasing basis. You can practise the presence of him and in doing so join him in accomplishing his mission in this world. It is to this subject that we now turn.

## 16. THE NEEDS AROUND US

About a year into his teaching ministry, Jesus decided to pay a visit to his home town of Nazareth. He'd been preaching the good news in one village after another, receiving rave reviews and seeing solid results: men, women and children by the scores were taking Jesus at his word and giving their lives to God. Dropping in on the community of people who reared him would probably just be the icing on the cake.

Jesus rose early on his first Saturday morning back in Nazareth and headed for the one place you'd expect to find the Son of God on the Sabbath: a house of worship. He entered the synagogue and was handed a rolled-up scroll that contained what we now know as the book of Isaiah. He unfurled it, scanned the page until he found the passage he'd come to share and then said,

> The Spirit of the Lord is on me,
>   because he has anointed me

> to preach good news to the poor.
> He has sent me to proclaim freedom for the prisoners
> and recovery of sight for the blind,
> to release the oppressed,
> to proclaim the year of the Lord's favour. (Luke 4:18–19)

Mind you, Jesus could have preached about absolutely anything on that particular day. And yet, when given centre stage, he chose to convey his Father's heart for resourcing the under-resourced.

Luke 4:16–21 says that after he'd finished, he rolled up the scroll, gave it back to the attendant and sat down. Which meant he'd been standing the entire time he taught. This is significant because Jesus was a rabbi, and when rabbis taught in those days, they never did so while standing. Teacher and congregation alike would rise to their feet when the rabbi quoted Scripture, but everyone quickly took their seats once things shifted to human commentary about what God had just said. Through his actions he asserted that he was God.

Then, as if this apparent rabble-rouser hadn't caused enough of a stir already, Jesus laid a comment on his audience that would elicit real shock. 'Today', he said, 'this scripture is fulfilled in your hearing' (Luke 4:21). In other words, everything the prophet Isaiah had said seven hundred years ago was about to be fulfilled right here and right now – before their Nazarene eyes.

As Jesus spoke these words from the Holy Scriptures, remember, he was looking into the eyes of people he knew quite well. He had grown up here. To put it in modern-day terms, Nazarene streets were where he and his friends had played football after school. It was to this crowd that he delivered, not just any message, but one that dealt with their coming Messiah.

He looked at the people he had hung around with since his days in nappies and in essence said, 'I'm the man. I am the man to which all of the Scriptures heretofore have been referring. When the Scriptures say the Messiah is going to do this or that, they're referring to me.

'My grand plan of redemption starts today. I'm going to forgive people of their sins and transform them by the power of my love. I'm going to mobilize every person who follows me to engage in the epic battle of establishing the kingdom of God here and now. And I'm going to invite what's working right in heaven to occur here on earth.

'Thy kingdom come, thy will be done, on earth as it is in heaven . . . remember that part of the prayer? I'm serious about it. On earth, thy will, O God, be done as it is in heaven. The things going on in heaven – the sincere worship, the active honouring of people, the living out of peace, all of it – I'm going to work to get all of that happening here.'

## Expectations and assumptions

Can you imagine what must have been whirring through the minds and hearts of Jesus' listeners that day? Could this really be their long-awaited Messiah?

'I'm here to enlist caring, compassionate people in this great struggle to merge heaven and earth,' Jesus may have said. 'I intend to motivate my followers to overturn the evil practices that keep poor people entangled in poverty, to overcome the systems that unjustly incarcerate people, sometimes just because of the colour of their skin. Together we will oust the systems that keep marginalized people from medical attention and health care, and we will upend every scheme that oppresses those who are weak and vulnerable.

'This grand struggle begins today. And now that you know my plan, I have a very important question to ask you: Will you rally around it, or will you reject it – and me – altogether?'

Most of the Jews hoped their coming Messiah would be a political deliverer, a military leader who could help them get Rome off their backs, or an economist astute enough to escort their beloved nation of Israel into unprecedented prosperity. But to their assumptions and expectations, Jesus essentially said, 'My main mission is not to fight Rome or to make you wealthy and happy in this life. My main mission is to free you from your sin and enlist you into waging war against the systems that consign people to poverty, disease, despair and hopelessness.'

It was a big pill for his listeners to swallow that day. So big, in fact, that a horde of people rebuffed Jesus and his heaven-and-earth ideas, dragged him out of the worship centre and resolved to throw the freshly discovered Messiah off a cliff. Not exactly the reception he had hoped for – but because he's God and they were not, he managed to get out of the near-fatal quandary unscathed.

## Your God-designed era

Still today, thinking about following Jesus Christ remains a big pill to swallow. When rational human beings consider committing themselves to the One whose main mission has always been to exercise compassion instead of power, to serve the poor instead of his own desires for wealth or possessions and to lift up the downtrodden instead of his own ego, even the best of us feel a little queasy at our own inadequacy.

Then, just as we get that pill down – the Jesus-is-adequate-and-we're-not pill – and submit ourselves to Christ's care, we come face to face with the unbelievable reality that he is committed to making us adequate too. In other words, following Christ doesn't just mean we bear his name; it also means we become transformed into his image.

In essence Jesus says, 'Look, between the day you say yes to me and the day you show up on heaven's doorstep, you can actually help me right what's wrong down here. You can care about the things I care about and in doing so find perfect peace, perfect satisfaction, perfect adequacy.

'You don't have to stay on your futile, self-help plan, build your own little kingdom and then someday, when you're old and grey and washed up, just die and go to heaven. Far from it! When you choose to follow me, you can enter into a God-designed era in your life where together we find your role in fixing this broken world. Certainly, you can look forward to eternal life in heaven. But between now and then, your earthly life can actually matter.'

When you join God's plan and begin to understand all that it entails, you find life in all its fullness. You see that being on a God-guided adventure truly is living life on another level than merely competing for the wealth and achievement and prizes and toys of this world. The Luke 4 passage reminds us that of course Christ wants his followers to point people who don't know him towards his gift of grace. But once they receive it, the goal should be inviting them to band together with other Christ-followers and get busy addressing the needs of the poor.

'We're going to set our agenda on those who are marginalized and those who are vulnerable and those who have no power and no voice,' Jesus reiterates. 'Friends, we're going to become their power and their voice. And we're going to lift them up, one life at a time. This is how heaven invades earth.'

## Called to pray

If I had to declare one topic that deserves more prayer from faithful prayers than any other in this day and age, it's this one – praying for the under-resourced all around us. I know, a lot vies for your attention, and it's easy to become consumed with your own needs as you pray. But it's hard to deny that when Jesus was given a platform, he used it, not for his own selfish gain, but rather to fight for those who were penniless and hopeless.

Jesus would say throughout his teaching that his followers would be marked by mercy. What would distinguish them from the non-followers is that their hearts would race for people in need. Their hands would wrestle for resources that they could then give away. Their wallets would reflect sacrificial stretching to meet people's needs instead of settling for doling out five pounds here and there. Their minds would work diligently to wrap themselves around the real issues under-resourced people face.

'My followers', Jesus would teach, 'are going to fight for the poor.' And based on my experience, this God-enabled fighting spirit shows up only when I am down on my knees. When I am alone with God and truly seek his will for how I am to respond to the vast needs that surround me, that's when the power of prayer hits home with me.

In those moments I see the devastating brokenness God sees. I am reminded of the tremendous blessings God has afforded me. And as I convey my heart and listen for his promptings, I find myself committed afresh to helping him fix a few things. But it all starts with pondering – really pondering – the plight of the poor.

### Barely scraping by

An intelligent, highly trained and accomplished writer named Barbara Ehrenreich wrote a book several years ago entitled *Nickel and Dimed*, which laid out the agonizing realities faced by a class of people in the States called the 'working poor'. Ehrenreich hid her professional pedigree, packed her bags and set out undercover on a year-long trek to experience what the working poor in many cases go through their entire lives. She spent three or four months at a time in places like Florida, Maine and Minnesota, and in each location she tried to carve out a decent existence for herself by working at entry-level jobs.

Within a month of accepting her first role – waitress at one of those restaurants that's connected to a bargain motel – her mind was blown by the same dynamic that is disillusioning millions of Americans these days. She discovered that a person can work honestly and diligently at a forty-hour-a-week job at entry-level pay with a decent employer and still wind up having no food, no shelter and no hope for assistance any time soon.

Ehrenreich discovered that the economic maths that once worked in many parts of the United States is no longer working. Monthly wages earned by entry-level employees are no longer sufficient to allow for the rental of a one-bedroom apartment in the area where you work, not to mention the purchase of nutritional groceries in order to maintain a healthy diet. Minimum wages probably won't give you the earning power to buy a used car or to purchase new clothing or toiletries or over-the-counter medicines, let alone build up a little emergency fund for when trouble hits or save for the down payment on a house to call your own.

Realizing she couldn't make ends meet with her nine-to-five job, Ehrenreich filled in the gaps by logging additional hours at the weekends with part-time jobs. It was interesting to her that often the companies that employed her were raking in profits to the tune of hundreds of millions of dollars, while their entry-level employees had no medical benefits, no transportation, no ability to save or invest, and substandard schools in their communities to ship their kids off to. Ironically, many leaders who earn high wages and have great influence in the corporate world don't know – or perhaps don't care – that urban poverty is a reality and that some of their own employees are barely scraping by.

## Living it out

From what the book of Luke tells us about the purpose and the mission of Jesus, near the top of his list was the goal of transforming the structures and the systems in society that drain the hope out of people who are doing what society tells them they ought to do and yet are still surviving just north of despair. I once met the owner of a dynamic business who really understood this.

Earlier in his life he had been shell-shocked by a personal encounter with Jesus Christ. When I met him, he was part of a solid church that did a balanced job of teaching about Christianity, including educating its members on the plight of the poor. On more than one occasion his conscience had been pricked regarding his responsibility to the poor as a Christian leader in the marketplace.

One day, after one of those sermons where his world was rocked by the power of Christ's teaching on this subject matter, he prayed to God and asked what he should do. In response he received a prompting he believes came directly from the Holy Spirit. The following week he went to work and invited a group of his minimum-wage earners to help him with a survey he wanted to conduct. The main question he asked them was a simple one: 'What quality of life can you sustain, based on the wages you earn from working at my company?'

The answers appalled him. The entry-level workers in his company could not afford to live anywhere near the company's offices and could not afford the basic necessities of life, such as food and clothing.

Later that week he called an emergency meeting with his finance team. 'I'm commissioning you to conduct a formal study of this community's true cost of living – apartment rental fees, starter home costs, mortgage rates, food totals, utility totals, transportation totals and school-related expenses. I want to see it all.'

It took his team several months to complete the task, but finally the information was assembled. He analysed every figure and then went back to his finance chief. 'Now I want you to calculate the hourly pay rate necessary for our entry-level workers to have the kind of life they deserve. What do we need to pay them so they can do more than merely make ends meet?'

To this Christian businessman's credit, and in deference to the teaching of Christ, he defied business logic, established a whole new economic model for his company and raised the minimum wage for his workers far above the national mandate. The decision lifted an entire entry-level workforce out of despair.

I heard about this man's boldness and was so impressed that I arranged a meeting with him. When I asked why he did what he did, he said words I'll never forget: 'If I talk it on Sunday, I've got to walk it on Monday to Friday. If I sit in a church and sing that Christ means a lot to me, if I read a Bible and agree with the preaching of my pastor, I'd better live it out. It's what Jesus taught us to do.'

I thought that was one of the finest things I had ever heard. But again it all traced back to a humbling moment before the God of the universe when one Christ-follower fell to his knees and with a sincere heart asked, 'How can one person make an impact on something as big as the generation-spanning plight of the poor? What's mine to do, Lord?' Then, upon receiving God's answer, that one Christ-follower took action.

A little later, in Luke 12:48, Jesus taught that of the one to whom much is given – be it influence or resource or power – much is required. I wonder how many of us ponder the vast gifts God has given us and how we are to steward them as a result. I wonder if the Spirit of God isn't whispering to us that there is something we can do, a role for us to play.

Maybe, just maybe, God has resourced us for reasons that go far beyond our own comfort and stability. Maybe we're in the enviable position we're in so that we can be used by Christ to lift up the downtrodden, even at the place of our own employment. That's something we could think about. That's something that we might be able to do. The question that remains is, will we fall to our knees and ask the questions too? Moreover, will we be brave enough to act on God's answer?

## A formula for disaster

Being part of the working poor is an atrocious place to be. But there is a state of affairs worse still. More than two-thirds of the people in our world are living in what can only be classified as extreme poverty. Instead of reflecting heaven coming down to earth, this looks and smells and feels more like hell coming up.

I went to sub-Saharan Africa recently to do a film about the HIV/AIDS crisis and some of the work Willow has been engaged in to alleviate suffering there. As the crew and I made our way from one location to another, I found my mind drifting off-task to the awful realities faced by these villagers. I couldn't shut off my thoughts as I looked at the bare feet and bloated bellies and sullen eyes surrounding me. 'What is it about this place that has such a vice-like grip on my soul?' I wondered.

It was extreme poverty, plain and simple. And as I think about it more these days, I sense in my spirit greater and greater levels of urgency – and ferocity – about eradicating it in all its hideous forms. For starters, in extreme poverty, every minute of every day is shrouded by a state of non-stop hunger.

Days after I returned from Africa, I had a stopover on a domestic trip and wound up sitting in a lounge in some airport for several hours. There was a nice enough chap sitting next to me, and to pass time we made small talk. I don't remember anything about the conversation except for one comment he made. 'I was just on a flight from Chicago to Dallas that didn't serve any food. Can you believe that? I'm so hungry I'm going to die!'

I looked at him incredulously. It's only a ninety-minute flight! And eyeing the extra forty pounds of freight he was carrying, I thought, 'You could fly a long time without food, my friend, and your body would probably thank you for the reprieve!' I had just come out of an environment where people were literally dying from lack of food, and here's someone moaning and groaning because he can't survive an hour and a half without being fed a meal. Talk about opposing realities!

We don't know this world of poverty. We try to get our arms around it, but we just can't comprehend what it is like.

A couple of years ago I watched a television special featuring a reporter who was studying poverty and the long-term effects of hunger. He interviewed a man who had lived in a state of hunger for his entire life. Wanting to grasp what this must have been like, the reporter said boldly, 'I'm going to live your life for thirty days. I'm going to eat exactly what you eat and drink exactly what you drink for thirty days straight.'

On day twenty-one this reporter had to bail out. He was dizzy, he was faint and he couldn't function. His mind had slowed down and his body had begun to waste away. He just couldn't take it.

Twenty-one days. This other man had lived this way for

forty-plus years, and someone pretty much like me had lasted less than a month. We simply cannot relate to what billions of people on planet Earth today are facing in this regard. Billions.

But it's more than merely a food crisis. Extreme poverty also involves shelter, or the lack thereof. I was in Cairo some time ago, and as I walked down the street, I noticed a burned-out car lying on its top, right there on the pavement. I looked around, questioning in my own mind why the city workers hadn't dragged the unsightly mess away. I walked around to the other side of the car and discovered why: there was a family living in it.

On another occasion I was in India and saw that Mumbai officials were putting in a new sewage system in one part of town. There were sewer pipes strewn along major roadways, waiting to be installed. But for now they were serving as an eight-foot-circumference 'Home, Sweet Home' for hundreds of families. I wrestled with the logic until I realized that those pipes were probably a far better shelter than where those families had lived beforehand.

And then there is sanitation. During one of the morning shoots on the trip to Africa I mentioned, just as we began taping, I saw a young mother emerge from her thatch-roofed hut. Her children trailed her, all three caked in dust and dirt and grime. The only thing I could think about was how it was eight o'clock in the morning, these children were just now setting foot outside and already they were a filthy mess.

The nearest water source was more than mile's walk from her home, so understandably she didn't get to the laundry the night before. Who knows how long it had been since her children's tattered clothes had been washed? I'd go mad without a daily shower, and yet who knows how long it had been since she and her family had had the dignity of being clean?

But it doesn't end there. Try receiving medical treatment when you're entrenched in extreme poverty. I've been reading about this issue lately, and the numbers blow my mind. There are far too many children dying every day of diarrhoea – a condition that is solvable with a pill that costs pennies. Hundreds of thousands of children will never see adulthood just because we can't figure out a fair distribution of medical supplies. It's deplorable.

Or try getting an education. Talk about injustice! Countless children are denied schooling simply because they can't afford a uniform or school supplies required by law to attend.

Or economic opportunity. Of the six billion people in the world, three billion – one half of humanity – live on less than one pound a day. What's more, they have no access to capital, so they cannot apply for and receive a loan that would dislodge them from their pitiful reality.

Friend, what I describe is the very real world where people live. For those who are left-brained, I worked out what this world looks like in equation form. Are you ready for this? Here is the equation:

EP + X = AM

EP stands for extreme poverty, which we've just explored. Now, in addition to EP, you add X to the equation. X might be HIV / AIDS. It might be famine. It might be civil war, as in the Democratic Republic of Congo, where according to the International Rescue Committee nearly four million people have died in the last ten years. This is in one country, mind you. Four million people have died in the Democratic Republic of Congo, and the world doesn't even know about it.

Some would say that part of the reason why the world doesn't know and doesn't care is because this atrocity is happening to black people who are out of sight and out of mind. If they were Europeans, it would be front-page news in every paper, every day.

The point I'm making is that when you add the X of incurable disease or famine or war or natural catastrophe – floods, hurricanes and so forth – to extreme poverty, it equals AM, or abject misery. Abject misery is a level of daily suffering that boggles the human mind. But when you accept it as reality, you achieve what I consider a graduate-level understanding of the plight of the poor.

## An antidote for shrivelled souls

On the heels of my Africa experience, I came across a book by Bryant Myers entitled *Walking with the Poor*. He would tell you that, as bad as my equation is, there's another element that makes matters even worse. Myers contends that when people have lived only in abject misery, they begin to operate from a marred identity. Over time, then, the equation looks like this:

EP + X = AM + MI

Marred identity is the internalization of external misery. People who have known nothing but the horrors of extreme poverty begin to believe that they actually deserve their devastating circumstances. They believe that the powers that be or the gods of fate have relegated them to this way of life and that there is nothing they or anybody else can do to change their lot in life. The more they wrestle with marred identity, the faster they sink into listlessness, lifelessness and a form of hopelessness that is palpable for everyone who observes them.

As I have made my way through villages in places like Zambia and South Africa, I've seen in the vacant eyes and in the warped posture of men, women and children a kind of resignation I honestly didn't know existed. I have heard despair in their flat voices when they respond to the good news of Jesus Christ, because any good news they may ever have known died in them decades ago. Inside these emaciated bodies all that remains is this marred identity – lives so damaged that, apart from a supernatural work of God, their souls will shrivel a little more every day of their misery-filled existence until at last they give way to the struggle.

I have no way of knowing what words like these do to you, but if you could see the kind of thing I am describing – and perhaps you have seen it – it would utterly wreck you. If you have a heart at all, something would shift inside you, never to return to its previous state.

I know this from personal experience. I have been travelling to Third World countries for twenty-five years, but the last time I went (I don't know if it's because God has me in a different condition these days or what) something in me got turned upside-down, and I just can't get back to where I was before.

It helps me understand with greater clarity why, when Jesus launched his ministry, he said that he and his followers were going to confront the structures and the systems and the people that work together in darkness of mind and spirit to keep those who are poor entangled in poverty.

He said, 'We're going to announce some good news to those people who are very close to having a marred identity. And we're going to work until the sun goes down on this world's existence to let a certain group of people know that they are not forgotten, they are not damaged goods, they are not hopeless and they are not beyond the possibility of being loved by our great God and by his followers.'

Jesus Christ identified with the poor in the manner in

which he lived. He associated with the poor and hung out with them often. He healed those who had no recourse to medicine. He fed the hungry by the thousands. And he said to those with marred identities, 'You're treasured creations of the Most High God. I will redeem you and call you my own.'

But the most important thing Jesus did is call his followers to join him in fixing this broken world – to join him in the epic struggle to bring what's going on in heaven down to planet Earth.

## It starts with prayer

No doubt about it, the brokenness can become overwhelming. These days, we're living in the presence of unthinkable societal ills and disease, corporate corruption and greed, family structures that have been blown up by affairs and domestic violence and emotional abuse, and the list goes on and on with issues that spin our heads and splinter our hearts.

But for the Christ-follower, the truth of the matter is that we're also living in the presence of God. And if ever there were a time for God's people to take up residence in his presence fully and completely, it is now.

Get before God, my friend. Ask him to give you his eyes to see, his ears to hear, his mind to think wisely. Ask him to usher you into your God-designed era for helping to fix all that's wrong in this very wrong world. He will be faithful to answer you and to guide you. He will provide peace so that you can live in the midst of darkness with unquenchable light. And he will provide power so that your life will count between now and an eternity spent by his side.

# QUESTIONS FOR REFLECTION AND DISCUSSION

## Chapter 1: God of peace, God of power

1. What difference does prayer make in your life?
2. How can prayer sometimes seem to impose on our individuality?
3. What draws you to prayer?
4. What causes you to resist praying?
5. What is the relationship between prayer and God's power? How does this concept relate to Romans 8:26?
6. When have you experienced God's power through prayer, such as seeing practical needs met, obstacles removed or problems solved?
7. List some of the underlying questions you have concerning prayer.
8. How would you like to see your communication with God improve as you study this book?

## Chapter 2: God is willing

1. Do you feel comfortable or uncomfortable in going to God with your problems? Explain.
2. How does Bill Hybels' interpretation of the story of the widow and the judge (Luke 18:2–8) affect your

attitude towards prayer?

3. What factors cause you to think that God is unwilling to respond to your prayers?
4. After reading this chapter, what makes you think that God is naturally generous?
5. When do you have a hard time accepting God's gifts to you? Why?
6. When you think of God's generosity, how often do your thoughts centre on material blessings? Why?
7. What parallels can you draw between God's generosity to us and parents' generosity to their children?

## Chapter 3: God is able

1. Do you bring your deepest needs to God every day? Why or why not?
2. While some Christians believe God is willing to answer prayer, inwardly they question God's ability to do so. What would cause Christians to question God's ability?
3. What factors might keep God from working his will in the world?
4. How might an inadequate view of God affect our prayer lives?
5. In the depths of your heart, do you believe God has the power to solve your problems? Why or why not?
6. Is it easier for you to go to God with small prayer requests or major requests? Why?
7. Do you think that first-century Christians were more inclined to believe in God's power than Christians do today? Explain.
8. What is the relationship between prayer and faith? Read Hebrews 11:1, 8–18 and describe how faith might affect the content of our prayers.
9. How could you make your prayers more sincere?

## Chapter 4: Heart-building habits

1. How do you respond to Bill Hybels' statement, 'Our spirits, like our bodies, have requirements for health and growth'?
2. Name some habits that contribute to spiritual health. Are these habits part of your life?
3. What are the warning signs of a straitjacket approach to discipline?
4. Why shouldn't we just 'go with the spiritual flow', as described on page 49?
5. Are you a list maker or a free spirit? How has this affected your prayer life?
6. What decision needs to be made by everyone who is serious about growing a strong prayer life?
7. List Jesus' four prayer principles as laid out for the disciples in Matthew 6:5–13.

## Chapter 5: Praying like Jesus

1. What priority did Jesus place on prayer? How do we know this?
2. What priority do you place on prayer? How do you show this?
3. What are the advantages of seeking out a private location for prayer?
4. How might creating a special atmosphere for your daily prayer time improve your talks with God?
5. How might you benefit from writing out your prayers?
6. Do you feel that a written prayer has disadvantages? Explain.
7. How sincere are you in your prayers? How much of your prayer life consists of empty, shallow phrases as opposed to deep and genuine pleas?

8. How might you avoid the habit of using meaningless repetition in prayer?
9. Is it easier for you to pray in general terms rather than specific terms? If so, why do you suppose this is the case?

## Chapter 6: A pattern for prayer

1. What are the characteristics of an unbalanced prayer life?
2. Do you see the need to establish a prayer routine? Explain.
3. Bill Hybels uses the acrostic ACTS (adoration, confession, thanksgiving and supplication) to introduce us to a balanced prayer life. Which elements come easily to you? Which elements do you most often omit?
4. Why is it good to start your prayers with adoration?
5. Why do you think adoration is so often omitted from our prayer lives?
6. How do you adore God?
7. What are some benefits of confession?
8. What changes occur in your life when you deal with sin in specific terms?
9. What is the difference between being grateful and expressing thanks to God? Why does God ask us to express thanks?
10. What categories do your prayer requests fall under? Which category gets the most attention?

## Chapter 7: Mountain-moving prayer

1. How do you usually respond to difficulties in life?
2. In your prayers, how much of your time is spent focusing on your problems compared with the amount of time you spend focusing on God?

3. What keeps us from focusing our prayers more on God?
4. How does a focus on God change the way we see ourselves?
5. In what ways can we focus more on God in our prayer lives?
6. Are any 'immovable mountains' causing you to doubt God's power or care? Explain.
7. Do you think there are mountains that God allows to remain? How does that affect your prayers?

### Chapter 8: The hurt of unanswered prayer

1. What difficulties do you have with unanswered prayer?
2. What are some examples of inappropriate prayer requests we might make without even realizing it? Can you name some inappropriate prayer requests you have made?
3. Why might God delay answering a prayer request?
4. In what ways have you coped with the problem of unanswered prayer in the past?
5. When can you recall instances where the timing of your prayer request was wrong?
6. What are the typical motives behind your prayer requests?
7. How does our living in an 'instant' society affect our prayer lives?
8. If some of your prayers don't seem to fit into the no/slow/grow categories, what other reasons might there be for unanswered prayer?

### Chapter 9: Prayer busters

1. What most motivates you to develop your prayer life?
2. What most hinders the development of your prayer life?
3. What are the 'prayer busters' Bill Hybels identifies in

this chapter? Can you identify some additional prayer busters?

4. How can unresolved relational conflict affect our prayer lives?
5. Can you recall some selfish prayer requests? Explain.
6. In what ways can we try to manipulate God by offering self-serving prayers?
7. Do you have trouble remembering to pray for Christians around the world? Why do we often have trouble praying for those we do not know personally?
8. What are a few 'worthy activities' you might be substituting for prayer? Why is it so easy to fall into this trap?
9. If your prayers aren't answered, do you tend to blame yourself? Why or why not?
10. Consider the story of Job. Was Job's misfortune his own fault? Is God's first concern always to answer prayer?

## Chapter 10: Cooling off on prayer

1. What was prayer like for you when you first became serious about praying?
2. When have you ever experienced a cooling-off period in your prayer life? What do you suppose caused it?
3. Bill Hybels says, 'One reason why we stop praying or let our prayer lives fade is that we are too comfortable.' Do you agree? When have you been too comfortable to pray?
4. When have you been driven to prayer because of serious problems you were facing? Did you continue to pray after the problems were solved?
5. Have you put a time and place for prayer in your daily schedule? When and where do you pray?
6. When has guilt kept you from praying? At the time, did

you realize how your sin was affecting your time with God?

7. What kinds of cheating were going on in Malachi's day? How do we cheat in those categories today?
8. How can we break down the guilt barrier and restore our relationship with God?
9. How long should we persist in praying for apparently hopeless cases?

## Chapter 11: Slowing down to pray

1. Make a list of the activities that filled your time during the past week. In what ways are you investing your time wisely, and in what ways are you simply overcommitted?
2. Do you truly believe that prayer is a profitable use of your time? Explain.
3. What does Bill Hybels mean by 'authentic Christianity'?
4. Where does God's still, small voice fit into your hectic schedule?
5. What are some of the benefits of keeping a journal?
6. If you have tried to keep a journal in the past, what difficulties or benefits have you encountered?
7. Do you feel that the act of writing out your prayers would be helpful? Restrictive? Explain.
8. What would keep you from writing out your prayers? How could you overcome these obstacles?

## Chapter 12: The importance of listening

1. Does God speak to you? If so, how?
2. Do you think of prayer primarily as you talking to God or as God talking to you? Explain.
3. What reasons does Bill Hybels give for listening to God? Do you have any additional reasons?
4. What part does listening to God play in your prayer life?

5. Do you believe listening to God can be carried to extremes? What are some of the misguided approaches Hybels lists? What other extremes would you consider dangerous?
6. Why is it important to be interested in the Holy Spirit's leading in your life?
7. What is the relationship between Christian growth and responding to God's leading?
8. Why is it important to be interested in the Holy Spirit's leading in your life?

**Chapter 13: How to hear God's promptings**

1. What factors keep us from hearing God's voice?
2. What are some benefits that come from the discipline of solitude?
3. How can solitude become intimidating to you?
4. How much time do you set aside in your prayer life for allowing God to speak to you?
5. Why do you feel that Christians fail to hear God's voice more often?
6. How could you better organize your prayer time to give God more opportunities to speak to you?
7. What is your reaction when you listen for God's voice but get no response?

**Chapter 14: What to do with promptings**

1. Why are we often reluctant to respond when we receive a prompting from God?
2. How can we be sure that a prompting is from God? Could it be our own desires? A temptation from Satan? How can we know the difference?
3. How do you usually respond to the promptings you receive from God?

4. Have you ever responded to a prompting that turned out to be false? What was the result?
5. What part does the Bible play in relationship to promptings from God?
6. Do you think God would lead us into an area where we are not gifted? Why or why not?
7. Has God more often led you to serve others or to be served? Explain.
8. What cautions must we exercise in trying to discern God's promptings in our lives?
9. When we listen for God's promptings, do we need to know why God is asking us to do something? Why or why not?
10. How do you feel when it seems God is silent?

### Chapter 15: Living in God's presence

1. What is the relationship between prayer and living in the presence of God?
2. Is it easier for you to speak with God from a rational or an experiential perspective? Explain.
3. How has God revealed his presence throughout history?
4. Does God reveal his presence to us today? If so, how is this presence different from God's presence in Bible times? How is it similar?
5. How can we practise the presence of God in our lives?
6. What benefits come from practising the presence of God?
7. What would it take to transform the times when you wash dishes or mow the lawn into an opportunity to commune with God?
8. What is the most important insight you have gained from your study of prayer thus far?

## Chapter 16: The needs around us

1. Why do you suppose Jesus chose to preach about the poor when he was given the opportunity?
2. Why were the Jews devastated when they learned that their Messiah wasn't whom they thought he would be? Throughout your own spiritual journey, what types of 'boxes' have you tried to fit Jesus into?
3. Have you ever considered that part of your life's purpose is to help Jesus put right what's wrong in the world? Why or why not?
4. Why do so many of us stay on a self-help plan even after we say we've surrendered our lives to Christ?
5. Have you ever been prompted to pray for the plight of the poor? Why don't more of us engage in regular prayer of this type?
6. Would you ever take on the life of a poor person, as Barbara Ehrenreich volunteered to do? Why or why not? If so, what do you think you might learn in the process? If not, what are the biggest fears or obstacles that would keep you from doing so?
7. What might it look like in your life to 'talk it on Sunday and walk it on Monday to Friday'?
8. Have you ever prayed the prayer, 'What's mine to do, Lord?' Might you be willing to pray it now?
9. How did Bill Hybels' definitions of 'extreme poverty' affect your understanding of the subject? Have you ever known people suffering in extreme poverty? If so, how would you describe the challenges they face?
10. What type of poverty do you see around you in your day-to-day life? How might your prayers make a difference?

## A GUIDE FOR PRIVATE OR GROUP PRAYER

**Adoration: entering holy space**
Read or sing one of these psalms of praise, or another of your choosing (such as Psalms 8; 19; 23; 46; 100; 148; Luke 1:46–55, 68–79; Ephesians 1:3–14).

Come, let us sing for joy to the LORD;
let us shout aloud to the Rock of our salvation.
Let us come before him with thanksgiving
and extol him with music and song.
For the LORD is the great God,
the great King above all gods.
In his hand are the depths of the earth,
and the mountain peaks belong to him.
The sea is his, for he made it,
and his hands formed the dry land.
Come, let us bow down in worship,
let us kneel before the LORD our Maker;
for he is our God
and we are the people of his pasture,
the flock under his care. (Psalm 95:1–7)

Holy, holy, holy
is the Lord God Almighty,
who was, and is, and is to come . . .
You are worthy, our Lord and God,
to receive glory and honour and power,
for you created all things,
and by your will they were created
and have their being . . .
Worthy is the Lamb, who was slain,
to receive power and wealth and wisdom and strength
and honour and glory and praise! . . .
To him who sits on the throne and to the Lamb
be praise and honour and glory and power,
for ever and ever! (Revelation 4:8, 11; 5:12–13)

I worship you and praise you because you are . . .

## Confession: naming our faults

If we confess our sins, he is faithful and just and will forgive us our sins and purify us from all unrighteousness. (1 John 1:9)

I confess that I . . .
I need your forgiveness for the sin of . . .

Please give me your strength
to forsake that sin
to make restitution by . . .
to accept your forgiveness and the new life you give me

I am in Christ!
I am a new creation!
The old has gone,

the new has come!
(see 2 Corinthians 5:17)

## Thanksgiving: expressing gratitude

Give thanks in all circumstances, for this is God's will for you in Christ Jesus.
(1 Thessalonians 5:18)

I praise you and I thank you
for answered prayers . . .
for spiritual blessings . . .
for relational blessings . . .
for material blessings . . .
for . . .

Praise be to the LORD,
for he has heard my cry for mercy.
The LORD is my strength and my shield;
my heart trusts in him, and I am helped.
My heart leaps for joy
and I will give thanks to him in song. (Psalm 28:6–7)

## Supplication: asking for help

Do not be anxious about anything, but in everything, by prayer and petition, with thanksgiving, present your requests to God.
(Philippians 4:6)

Here are my requests
for other people – family, friends, acquaintances, colleagues, people in my church, people in the news . . .
for myself – my work, my character, my health, my joys and sorrows . . .
for . . .

> Cast all your anxiety on him because he cares for you.
> (1 Peter 5:7)

Glory be to the Father and to the Son and to the Holy Spirit. As it was in the beginning, is now and ever shall be, world without end. Amen.